For my dear friends
Cynrie and Dave Weinberger
With warm regards –
Rabbi Alexander Alan Steinbach
Hannukah 1958

FAITH AND LOVE

OTHER BOOKS BY
ALEXANDER ALAN STEINBACH

When Dreamers Build
A Volume of Poems

Treatise Baba Mezia
(Co-author)

Sabbath Queen

What Is Judaism?

Musings and Meditations

In Search of the Permanent

Bitter-Sweet

ALEXANDER ALAN STEINBACH

AITH

AND

OVE

PHILOSOPHICAL LIBRARY
New York

Type set by *The Polyglot Press*, New York

Manufactured in the United States of America

To my Grandsons

Andrew Ira and Douglas Lloyd Greenspan

CONTENTS

FAITH AND LOVE

INTRODUCTION

Our age is not so far removed from Shakespeare's day that we cannot echo his panegyric: "What a piece of work is man! How noble in reason! how infinite in faculty . . . how like an angel, in apprehension how like a god!" By the same token, we cannot dismiss the contrary picture of man limned by Hamlet: "And yet, to me, what is this quintessence of dust?"

Contemporary events seem to corroborate Hamlet's skeptical view. The atomic age finds humanity fearful and petulant, insecure and suspicious. World conscience has sunk into eclipse. The earth's highways and byways are cluttered with masses of mankind in quest of the meretricious and the transient. The modern Adam is in danger of forfeiting his fruitful Garden of Eden.

At least part of the world's turmoil and distraction may be traced to the lamentable fact that many fundamental values have of late been obscured. The storms that have swept the international scene have left dreary trails of moral and spiritual desolation. The heart of civilization has been deeply scarred. Multitudes, beguiled by the allurements of material goals, find themselves tragically empty.

These essays have been written with the earnest hope that they might reach individuals in that numerous company who are groping for standards and direction. There are many who refuse to surrender to the tyranny of negation and despair, but they need a spiritual compass to illumine their way. The author is hopeful that these creations, by diffusing light into the mystery of life's harmonies and dissonances, may point the way to the restoration of man's confidence in himself.

Some of these essays have appeared in abbreviated form as editorials in *The Messenger*, published monthly by Temple Ahavath Sholom of Brooklyn, of which the author is senior Rabbi. Additional essays were specially written in order to complete this collection, and while each essay is a unit in itself, the entire collection presents a continuity of thought and of subject-matter. It purposes to help the reader build a platform upon which to rise toward a deeper knowledge of Faith and Love.

Alexander Alan Steinbach

OD, the celestial Gardener, implants two sublime perennials, Faith and Love, in every human heart-garden. These twin blossoms are nurtured by the sheen of Divinity streaming through the open windows of the soul. They are spiritual oracles that serve as intermediators between God who calls and the soul that answers. He who obeys that call is assured an uninterrupted influx of God's presence into the very core of his life. Love is God's voice; Faith is man's answer.

Faith and Love are not easy or casual attainments. They derive from the interplay of every facet in a human being: his mind and brain, his reason and emotions, his intuition and will. They represent precious ores that must be mined laboriously and patiently out of life's soul-quarry.

This task is not without its arduous demands. It requires a continuous and sometimes toilsome climb toward the peak where we may stand face to face with our noblest self. The ascent is frequently fraught with wearying and formidable obstacles, but Faith and Love serve as an invincible armor to triumph over defeat. He whose existence is tabernacled upon these two durable pillars bears the authentic stamp of Divine architecture. It is as though he hears angels whispering to him the deepest secrets of man's ineffable companionship with his Creator.

What is Faith? What is Love?

Faith is the bridge we throw across the yawning chasm between hope and doubt, belief and cynicism. It is the imponderable that teaches the spirit how to realize its loftiest dimensions. It dares to defy defeat even when reinforcements seem far away. When the rainbow seems broken in half, Faith commands: Go out and repair it!

Faith is the spiritual mortar that preserves our moral stamina against the bludgeonings of failure and futility and hurt. It is a lamp that shines through our darkness, a dawn that gleams through the black forest of our lost illusions. Faith is the unsilenced voice that thunders a resounding "aye" to challenge life's arbitrary "nay." It is the capacity to cling to God's hand when His hand appears to have been withdrawn; it is a refusal to surrender.

Love, on the other hand, is complete surrender. Life's enduring triumph is to cultivate the courage to yield to a will higher than our own. In marriage it is the will of the beloved; in religion it is the will of God. Love is the seal of the Divine upon man's finite heart. It converts the heart into a hearth upon which glow the embers of affection kindled by another heart. Human love makes us one with a kindred spirit; Divine Love makes us one with God.

Love elevates us to a rung higher than Faith. Faith is the torch that lights the way; Love is the key that unlocks the Holy of Holies. Faith is the promise; Love is the fulfillment. Faith commands; Love obeys. Faith is the fuel; Love the fire that warms and illumines. Faith is the cathedral with wide open doors; Love is the altar on which we worship after we have entered the cathedral. Faith is the road; Love the destination. Faith is the heart kneeling in prayer; Love is the Divine answer to the prayer.

In our day, when the world-garden is being tragically disfigured and defaced by locust hordes of hatred, insecurity and distrust, it behooves every individual to nurture more tenderly the blooms of Faith and Love in his own heart-garden. Such a collective undertaking must of necessity become a barrier against the growing fields of weeds in international relations. Here is where the individual truly counts;

~§ 4 §~

here are two instruments capable of regenerating mankind. Each of us, accepting the stewardship of the purifying fires of Faith and Love, will help reduce to ashes the monstrous furnaces of enmity being stoked by evil forces. Through the cultivation of these blooms we shall cover the deep scars of man's conflicts. They will diffuse a radiance that will disclose God's footprints in our lives and in our world.

ICTOR HUGO wrote a poem every person should memorize and inscribe upon the scroll of his heart. It rhymes with the inexorable inner struggle an individual must face periodically in his effort to scale the promontory of life's aspirations. Here is an English translation of the poem:

"Be like a bird that, pausing in his flight
Awhile on boughs too slight,
Feels them give way beneath him and yet sings,
Knowing he has wings."

Those who have experienced the fever and torment of struggle understand well the meaning of these lines. We are driven and harried by an incorrigible acquisitive instinct; we strain to wrench from life as many victories as possible. We resolve to be strong and hope to become affluent, influential and highly respected, believing these attainments may be forged into instruments that will enable us to mine the precious ores of happiness and tranquillity. We seek to devise plans wherewith we may overcome obstacles barring our path to success, but lose sight of the fact that the crowning triumph is to discover and master our true self, our unique individuality. How many of us ever become aware how much of the unused self we carry with us? It is there, but we seldom put it to work.

The burden of this unused self brings intimations that something is wrong. We become conscious of an inner emptiness that is symptomatic of a soul sickness. While pursuing external goals we stray from the highway that leads to the mansion of our self. We are like the actors in the ancient Greek and Roman theatres. They always wore a mask, known as their *persona,* through which their voices came to the audience. The mask was their false personality; it concealed their true self. How many men and women today speak and act not through their individual pristine self, but through an actor's mask?

In the mansion of self we need neither mask nor disguise. There we can fraternize with solitude and not be lonely. More than the things we labor to acquire, we need desperately an inner bastion whither we may retreat and stand face to face with our whole self. Lacking such a sanctuary, one will sooner or later sadly discover that the bough on which his existence is perched is too slight to sustain his yearning for self-expansion and for self-fulfillment.

And yet, however slight the bough, the pilgrimage to one's self is never hopeless if he remembers he has wings. Across every life a pathway is hewn from mundane earth to aspiring heaven, from prosaic groping to celestial upreaching. Often the ascent seems too formidable, almost inaccessible. There are many falls and many bruises, many failures and many tears. There are dark valleys and arid deserts, jagged mountains and dangerous tempests. But the upward vision is never concealed from one who dares to be himself. Steep is the road; pitiless are the taunts and the jeers hurled at him who rises above the dumb, unthinking herd. But there is no choice. Either you become remorselessly yourself or you remain a tragic dwarf, unfruitful like a stunted cactus in a parched Sahara. Either you rise to the noblest level within you, or you grope in a circle, cheated of the things you ought to be but never quite become. In the struggle between our inner and our outer life-urges, we must don a mask if we journey only through the lower reaches of the ego. Once we discover its upper reaches, we discard the mask and play the uninhibited role that expresses our true individuality.

No star woos another star so fervently in the illimitable silences of night as flight woos wings poised to soar. Our dreams are our wings; but they are utterly useless unless they leap upward into doing. To accept the threadbare adage "Life is a dream," is to encrust the self with a layer of rigor mortis. Life is *not* a dream. Life is myself, yet greater than myself. Therefore, if I accept the lethal servitude of blind, parochial conformity, I thwart the divine potential that is stamped within me. My true self is part of the Divine Self, and how can I hope to explore the Divine if I do not traverse the deeps where I need not be an actor? Until I become relentlessly myself, I not only betray the past from which I came, but also the seeded future planted within me.

But there is one final task to be achieved. It is not enough merely to be myself; I must suffer my fellowman to be himself. Failing to recognize my obligation to him as a brother, I befoul the exalted pattern life has woven into me. If I do not help him lift his wings, or heal them when they are maimed, I am a false sentinel on the ramparts of civilized living. I must carve God out of my spiritual self; this is a cardinal law I cannot escape. But I must guard against self-idolization, and how can I better achieve such a goal than by aiding others to carve God out of their spiritual selves? If thus I seek myself, I will surely find what I am seeking.

CONTEMPORARY THINKER sagely remarked, "The world's work has always been done by men who have suffered pain or have taken pains." Man at a very early age becomes conversant with the language of pain. Even if he is not an apt pupil, he learns quickly that the road to worthwhile achievement is paved with numerous obstacles. He must be willing to sacrifice, to face odds and to toil without surcease for the cherished goals he covets. Emerson reminded us, "Whilst man sits on the cushion of advantage he goes to sleep; when he is pushed, tormented, defeated, he has a chance to learn something."

Recently, while listening to a recording of Tchaikowsky's entrancing Symphony No. 6 in B Minor (the *Pathetique*), I recalled reading in his biography that a week before he began this masterwork he had written to a friend, "My faith in myself is terribly shattered, and it seems that my role is ended." What suffering he must have endured to be driven to such a nihilistic view of himself and of his future! He was in his fifties at the time, and his hypersensitive nature was ready to surrender to the host of painful blows life had administered through the years. And yet, out of the darkness that had closed in on him he plucked musical firebrands from the ashes of his disappointments and kindled them into the *Pathetique*. This transfiguring symphony, expressing the poignant, soul-searching lament of a wounded spirit, might never have been created had not the composer suffered as he did.

It is not suggested here that we should seek life situations that inspire moods of dejection and defeat. Only a masochist would deliberately court such situations. But we should remember that pain is a normative component of human existence. Therefore, when pain becomes a sculptor carving, without benefit of anesthesia, patterns of anguish upon our hearts, we must do more than merely rile against it. To denounce the heartless sculptor is pointless. Rather, we must find the stamina and the wisdom to transform pain into a constructive blueprint. Rebellion against suffering is like a general waging war without an army. Defeat is inevitable.

The rational attitude towards human suffering is to accept it as a reality in life, as part of our human legacy no less than joy and gratification. To disavow this dowry is to deny life itself. Charles Lamb wrote, "Pain is life—the sharper, the more evidence of life." True indeed! Suffering is woven into the very warp and woof of our terrestrial existence. It is often, as in Tchaikowsky's experience, a lens that reveals truths garnered in no other way. We must concur in William Penn's cryptic theorem, "No pain, no palm; no thorns, no throne; no gall, no glory."

It may be pointed out that much of the world's grandeur through the ages has been contributed by intrepid individuals who suffered greatly, physically, emotionally and mentally. A considerable portion of our music, art and poetry is the creation of persons who had plunged into the lowest abysses of despair. The discipline of suffering is not without its permanent fruitage. What kind of a world would we have if there were no storms to buffet, no fears to overcome, no crags to scale, no tears to dry, no scars to bear? In such a world there could not have arisen the pensive music of Chopin, the epic poetry of Milton, the monumental sculpture of Michelangelo, the immortal painting of Rembrandt. Nor would we have received countless other benefactions bestowed by courageous souls deeply gashed and heavy laden with trials.

Pain must be included among our assets. However difficult it is to bear, it performs a vital function. It heightens our wisdom, it deepens our character. When its sting recedes, we grow conscious of a sweet inner calm. We are comforted by the assurance that, come light or shadows, pain or pleasure, heartache or hope, we shall have learned how to deal maturely with each in its place.

MANY storms rack this planet that domiciles us. Our individual lives, too, are lacerated by violent upheavals. The artillery of thunder bombarding a sultry sky is no more turbulent than tempests that vent their fury from time to time in our personal lives. The structure of a scream howling out of the throat of a raving wind differs little, if at all, from the anatomy of a groan agonizing out of a tortured heart. One is audibly savage, the other low and subdued. But both are kindred notes in one octave, minor chords in the treble clef of existence. Both express a melodic lament no other form of communication can adequately convey.

The art of living and the art of music are Siamese-twinned. Each is both a call and an answer to the other. Sometimes it is hard to ascertain where one begins and the other ends. Strange deeps within us beat time to the rhythmic cadence of a concerto, or sway in unison to the seraphic strains of a symphony. A cheer and a sigh, a burst of laughter and a flood of tears, a moan and an exultant paean, a cynical sneer and a tremulous prayer—all are musical bars inscribed upon the manuscript of human existence. Life itself is a wayward adagio, and we are the thralled musicians singing its notes into a chorus of laughing, sobbing and pain.

Everything God created is a chord in the divine harmony that governs the universe. The song of a throstle is a hyphen between the poetry of heaven and the prose of earth, and a nightingale is a lute upon which the heavens play their cosmic etudes. Ocean waves creeping in to nestle against the white sand are arias in the duet that harmonizes distant tides with nearby shores. Sea shells hum lullabies of the eternal sea, and man's heart intones an anthem of immortality for his own eternal soul.

Countless performers participate in Nature's unending orchestration. Man employs stringed instruments, flutes, woods and horns to voice his rhapsodies. Nature's instruments are too numerous to record. But whether in Nature or in man, whether sky-born or earth-tuned, the most powerful, the most far-reaching medium of communication is music.

The burning log in the fireplace, crackling when the heat mounts—is this not a form of music? Birds chirping their secrets to tree boughs, acorns diving to the ground with a thud, eagles flapping their avid wings against bow strings formed by air waves, raindrops tapping their notes upon a window-pane, breezes strumming leaves like tiny Eolian lyres —are not all these rhythmic measures in the universal chorale composed by the master Musician?

Our throbbing heartbeats, too, are intermezzos in the total composition. They are sharps and flats and naturals pulsating out of a vibrant life fugue. Every ache and scar, every joy and pleasure, every tear and laugh, every sorrow and gladness—all are needed instruments in the musical drama of life.

Things small and things large, things young and things old, things mysterious and things understood, the visible and the invisible, the near and the far, participate in the universal chorus. The full and the empty, the healed and the broken, the inscrutable silence of the desert and the strident cough of a volcano in convulsion, the waltz of dawn and the mazurka of twilight, the white vomit of winter and the petaled melody of summer; each produces its own unique music. Autumn weaving its exquisitely colored death shroud, the unborn robin breaking its blue prison shell, the stabbing cry of a mother giving birth, all are chords in the sublime harmony.

In things low there are also fragments of song. Out of the scum of lives bereft of the power to dream, out of the abyss of splintered hopes, out of the gnawing of stomachs hungering for bread—out of these, too, one can detect the intimations of a song forgotten. Nothing is without music; it is a script unending. Everything that is and everything that will be, the vibrant movement of land and of sea, the pulse that beats in heaven or trembles on earth—all echo the eternal tune that cannot be silenced.

A PRACTICAL IMMORTALITY

SINCE the days of the caveman, the human mind has been feverishly groping for some kind of evidence to support the hope that physical extinction is not the terminus of existence. Man has refused to believe that life burns out like a candle. He has therefore clung to immortality as a dogma, maintaining there is a separate existence for the soul. This belief has become his armor against the sovereignty of death. Mortality holds that the body, like rain, sinks into the ground, and the human frame, like the flower nourished by the rain, ultimately courts oblivion. But believers in the doctrine of immortality do not accept this as the last word. They insist that annihilation is not man's fate. Something of him or within him perdures, something intangible but very real that cannot be weighed by the scales of mortality. This idea has persisted in one form or another since the ancients first carved hieroglyphics on rocks and inscribed their signatures on the papyri of antiquity.

Aside from its theological implications, one may seriously question why mankind, coveting life so intensely, should be profoundly concerned with a state of being that is unthinkable without death. Why be so exercised over the imperishable when the price it demands is human perishability? There are untold millions for whom this deeply longed-for impractical tomorrow is far more important than the practical, living today. Whatever cargo they receive from the argosy of the present, is only a ferry crossing into the future. This life is for them only a refueling station for the road that is yet to be traversed.

Such a mental attitude poses a perplexing spiritual and psychological problem. If the present is only tentative, only a fragment of a larger and broader entity which is conditioned by our dying, the value of the present is necessarily of temporary significance. Such an approach to daily living is not only negative, it is haphazard. The present must be regarded as a whole in itself, not merely as a prologue. It must be lived as the highest and most meaningful adventure to which life can aspire. One need not be so cynical as Heine who declared, "It must require an inordinate share of vanity and presumption, after enjoying so much that is good and beautiful on earth, to ask the Lord for immortality in addition to it all." There is a greater challenge in the words of the late American Rabbi, Joel Blau, "I have no particular taste for post-mortem immortality. I am immortal now, while I am gloriously alive." What a splendid statement regarding *practical immortality*!

I do not subscribe to the Epicurean philosophy, "Eat, drink, be merry; for tomorrow we die." But I avouch the conviction that the enlargement of life must be effected while we are still cavorting under the sun. It cannot be postponed until we slumber beneath the ground. We are in immortality with every breath we take, with every thought we think, with every good we create. Immortality is, indeed, with us now. From this practical point of view, it cannot possibly be escaped. To harness our minds to some intangible steed that will leap with us, Pegasus like, across the borders of the Here, is a fanciful experience. But it is not always convincing.

Everything throbs with a broader life potential. The seed enlarges into a flower, bush or tree. The egg hatches into a living creature. The brook flows into the stream, the stream into the river, the river into the sea or ocean. Nothing is static. All things under heaven's roof are touched by this law of enlargement.

Human life is no exception. Having evolved through countless years from a speck of slime through a thousand gradations and variations, man becomes a filament of immortality the moment he is born. His existence is a channel through which immortality flows. Some day, after he has developed a fourth, a fifth and even sixth dimension, he will learn the secret of continuing life in more practical terms than he now envisions immortality. He may yet discover an interpretation of life immeasurably superior to the present belief that he must die in order to live.

ATCHERS who gaze in early spring or late fall into the dawn sky or into the purple cliffs of twilight, behold an awesome spectacle. They see birds by the hundreds of thousands winging northward in spring and southward in autumn, their feathered sails navigating like celestial mariners. Their wings can clearly be heard beating a rhythmic tattoo against the heights. These migrations are as old as history. The Biblical books of Job and Jeremiah speak about them. Aristotle discussed them. But neither then nor now, except for speculations by ornithologists who by no means are in agreement, has anyone satisfactorily explained these mysterious migratory journeys. Do the spring and autumn equinoxes whisper some inscrutable secret that sends these restless wanderers into the ethereal lanes, to traverse the same skyways their ancestors traveled before them?

Northern hemisphere birds obviously fly south in the fall to assure themselves of food and a favorable climate for the winter months. But why do they return north in the spring? It would be less complicated for them to stay in the warm climate the whole year long. Too, how do the birds find their way, especially species like the amazing golden plover which flies from Alaska across trackless ocean wastes to New Zealand, a distance of 7,800 miles, and the Arctic tern which flies 12,000 miles to reach his summer home in the Antarctic? More than one hundred summer species leave Canada and the United States and fly approximately 1,500 miles to winter in the West Indies and in Central or South America. The smallest of all birds, the ruby-throated hummingbird, although no bigger than a large moth, flies an incredible 500 miles across the Gulf of Mexico from the Gulf states to Yucatan. What road map do these species possess? What miraculous instinct sends them on their way to the summer and winter habitats nearly the same date year after year?

Is there something in the birds' reproductive system that reacts to the breeding cycle and impels them to get to their breeding task? Or can it be, as one school of ornithologists holds, "that the species of birds that now migrate originated in the north in winterless pre-Ice Age times. Thus, the spring flight north is a return to an ancestral home."

Whatever be the answers to these and like questions, we may safely observe that the wisdom instinctively acquired by birds has as yet not been mastered by man's vaunted intellect. Men grovel, forgetting it is their destiny to fly. The human spirit has been endowed with invisible wings, but a forthright analysis of our world situation today will clearly reveal that an upsoaring trend is conspicuously absent. Birds throw their little frail bodies into the path of biting winds, and embark upon peregrinations that test their stamina. Many fall by the wayside—storms, exhaustion and birds of prey take their toll. But nothing prevents them from proceeding upon their journey to their new "Ellis Island." They possess wings and must use them.

Modern man moves on wheels, not on wings. He welcomes any gadget that will give him more leisure. He reads books in capsule form; he learns about world events from a television set. He wants more wages for less work, and more goods for less effort. He needs a garage for his car, but does not feel incomplete without a nesting place for his spirit. He is the happy beneficiary of a longer lifespan, but does little or nothing to use the extra years for selfless purposes. He lives a longer but not a fuller life. He admires superior qualities in others, but is content with mediocrity in himself.

Man must learn how to use the wings of his higher self. His

gaze must be reoriented toward wider horizons beyond the narrow hilltops of life's physical frontiers. He must be willing to be buffeted by life's winds in order to be lifted above himself. This is the migration to which he is capable of responding. Upreaching will bring a new vision, and the new vision will inspire a greater sense of duty. Duty will strengthen a feeling of moral obligation, and in discharging his moral obligation he will become worthy of the only aristocracy that is genuine—the aristocracy of self-respect.

HUNGER is a primordial bequest, or instinct, every living thing inherits from Nature. It sometimes becomes wilder than the stab of a sub-zero North wind. It is the insistent goad that drives the earthworm wriggling through the dark pores of the earth and fruit blossoms upreaching for the sun. It propels the eel downward into the slimy caverns of the sea and the eagle upward over its mountain rock aerie.

Hunger is, of course, a primary motif in the Marxian doctrine of economics. According to that doctrine, the savage struggle for bread has converted mankind into two categories: wolves and sheep, the latter rendered helpless by the spawn of hunger. One need not necessarily become an apostle of Marxism to agree that hunger has played a tremendous role in human history. Many centuries ago a Babylonian Rabbi, Raba, quoted the proverb, "The hungry man has sixty toothaches when another smacks his lips."

It is noteworthy that the Bible contains numerous allusions to hunger and to famine. The earliest appears in the twelfth chapter of Genesis, where we read, "And there was a famine in the land; and Abram went down to Egypt to sojourn there, for the famine was grievous in the land." Here is one of the first reports in recorded history which describes a human being forced by hunger to surrender his home. Abram's son, Isaac, also experienced a famine in his day. In Genesis 26.1 we read, "And there was a famine in the land, besides the first famine that was in the days of Abraham." Jacob, Isaac's offspring, sent his sons into Egypt to purchase grain, because of the famine "which was sore in the land." The Book of Ruth opens with the verse, "And there was a famine in the land." In 2 Samuel 21.1 it is asserted, "And there was a famine in the days of David for three years," and in 2 Kings 6.25, "And there was a great famine in Samaria."

All the aforementioned famines were due, of course, to a dearth of rainfall and to the subsequent aridity that strangled the soil. But beyond their literal implication, these phenomena suggest a deeper meaning. In the infancy of man's history he received the admonition, "By the sweat of thy face shalt thou eat bread." Since that day the skirmish for food has not ceased to tax man's ingenuity. Indeed, there have been times when he reverted to the law of tooth and claw. But even while engaged in this perennial struggle, he became increasingly aware of the challenge to his higher self expressed in Deuteronomy, "Man doth not live by bread alone." He grew ever more conscious of hungers that food could not appease and of appetites unrelated to physical repasts. Indeed, this became the pattern that marked his long trek over the rocky highway from apehood to manhood. Climbing tortuous step by step, advancing inch by inch and foot by foot, moving forward and tumbling backward, agonizing upward and thrusting downward, his lamp at times flickering so low that the road itself was almost obscured, man has been impelled onward by the sheer hunger for higher goals. When he toiled for bread alone, the caveman within him was sovereign. When he elected to create better standards and to improve the species, it was Divinity breaking through. Between these two categories of hungers, the physical and the spiritual, the material and the intellectual, humanity has consistently and uniformly oscillated. The so-called Dark Age and Golden Age in history are mirrors of the type of hunger mankind succeeded in mastering.

This motif of hunger, not for bread but for nutriment to sate the deeper spiritual, esthetic and intellectual needs within us, is the hallmark of advancing civilization. Man has never before possessed such abundance and largess as enrich his life today. And yet, he has seldom, if ever, experienced so many hunger pangs as he now feels. Despite his incalculable acquisitions, loneliness and homelessness haunt him. Fear, insecurity and emptiness gnaw at the spirit and tug at the heart of millions of men, women and children the world over. Sumptuous indeed is the material banquet the least of us may enjoy. At our fingertips we have gadgets our forebears never dreamed about.

But all these feasts do not mitigate the restlessness and apprehensiveness that cast long, menacing shadows over our contemporary age. The craving within us is a reminder of the prophecy of Amos in the eighth century B.C.: "Behold the days come, saith the Lord God, that I will send a famine in the land; not a famine of bread nor a thirst for water, but of hearing the words of the Lord." We are now in the midst of that famine. There is a great despair in the world. Populations are no longer men, women and children; they are hungers and thirsts, yearnings and appetites, cluttering our cities, large and small.

Man comes into the world hungry and empty-handed. He begins his infancy empty-minded and empty-hearted. Gradually the little empty hands are filled through the bounty of elders. Parental love displaces the heart's emptiness, and bits of understanding infiltrate the growing mind. Knowledge, love, acquisitions, physical development—all increase until they add up to a veritable feast. There seems nothing to hunger for.

But no matter how rich the feast, cravings and longings remain. Parts of us attain satiety, but there is never satisfaction for the totality of our being. A sense of exile, a gnawing inner homelessness persists. The spectre of famine clings like a shadow to our hearts.

What is the meaning of this hunger? When can the soul's restlessness be expected to abate? Only when we come to realize that life is hunger, and hunger is life. One cannot subsist without the other. Their relationship is akin to that between body and soul. Unless there be a spiritual hunger throbbing in a man's existence, he is on his way to stagnation. "Hunger is the teacher of the arts and the bestower of inventions." Let the heart and spirit be unafraid of hunger pangs. Thorny is the road over which they require us to walk, but glorious are the goals they enable us to achieve.

BOOKSHOPS are frequented by two types of people. There are those who seek a certain book and come to buy it. Others do not come for any particular volume; they browse leisurely among the books until they find one that needs them. Such a book becomes a bosom friend.

Men's attitude toward life is often akin to this attitude toward books. For many, fullness of living is equated with the satisfying of their needs. They deem it a badge of failure to go unsated. To be weighted down with a burden of un-requited desires is regarded as a stigma of defeat. Indeed, our capricious age has succumbed to the delusion that the summit of achievement is reached when one is successful in providing for one's wants. To multiply experiences of self-gratification has become a devout quest for multitudes of men and women everywhere.

Such a philosophy, confined as it is to a narrow interpreta-tion of human experience, disregards the supreme challenge of life. To say "I need you" is to voice a carol articulated by the lips of one's longing. It may be prompted by an irrepres-sible throbbing that pulses out of one's loneliness and long-ing for companionship. But it is an incomplete chorus. Some-thing vital is lacking; significant notes are missing. It lacks the tunefulness of the heart theme that hymns, "I am needed by you." Without this theme, the need is merely a solitary island; once supplied with it, the heart becomes a mainland.

To need is to become aware of the hollows that brood out of one's inner emptiness. It is the shadow of the ego wander-ing like a nomad across a parched desert. But to be needed is to experience the rapture of bringing completion to another. The former is interested in self-fulfillment. The latter is concerned with unlocking the portals that guard the precious mansion of otherness. Paraphrasing a popular aphorism: To need is human, to be needed is divine.

The maturation of individuality is consummated when it transcends its personal needs and grows into a haven and sanctuary for the needs of another. Once this maturity is attained, the more one gives the more one receives. Thus to be needed is to become like the resurrection of spring in a life hemmed in by the piercing talons of winter. What worthier personal goal can life pursue? To be a prime necessity to someone or to something is to establish a high orbit around which our noblest aspirations may revolve. Many days of our years will clutter like jetsam along the narrowing shores of our existence. The flagons of memory will be drained of the wine of dreams. But if we kindle a beacon to illumine a pathway leading to and from another, we shall become a benediction to one or to many who might otherwise be groping in canyons of loneliness.

Self-preservation is a natural and compelling instinct in our lives. Self-interest is a spontaneous by-product of the tyrannical spell our acquisitive instinct casts over us. It stirs within us a frenzied appetite for many things within reach. Crop after crop of needs cry out to be harvested. What the eye sees the hand wants to acquire. "To possess" becomes the password that goads us on.

One of the achievements of civilization is the conquest of man's acquisitive instinct. The yearning "to possess" must be counterbalanced by a willingness "to be possessed." If I am for myself and no more, I am the victim of a hardened egotism that leaves little room within me for anything except my "I." Whittier sagely observed:

> Heaven's gate is shut to him who comes alone,
> Save thou a soul, and it shall save thine own.

If I develop myself into a tributary flowing into another self, I become more than the self I originally possessed. The measure of my progress is, therefore, determined not by how much I need, but by how much I am needed. My brief existence may be like the passing of a raven's shadow across a greening field, but if something within me becomes part of someone outside me, I shall remain a fertile field even after I am gone.

NE seldom reflects upon the wonder of language, which is the most formidable weapon in the armory of the human mind. It is, of course, the medium through which we communicate, either orally or in writing, our thoughts and ideas. It is a precious reservoir in which the fruits of lightning flashes of genius have been safely stored and preserved through the ages. But a closer examination will reveal that language is infinitely more than a matter of words. There are depths of speech which words alone are impotent to convey.

Take music, for example. Here is a superb language that probably predates the emergence of the spoken word. Says Richter, "Music is the only one of the fine arts in which not only man, but all other animals, have a common property —mice and elephants, spiders and birds." It might be added that the "music of the spheres" preceded by billions of years the first song that came from human vocal organs.

Notes are the vocabulary in the language of music. The composer is enthralled by the irresistible sweep of his inspiration. The tonal speech he creates is intended for many ears, and for a period beyond his own. His "I" expresses itself as monologue, but it does not cease there. It embarks upon a search for "the other" who will hear his music. When his "I" finds a "thou," the monologue becomes dialogue, and fulfills the higher mission music is intended to serve. Whereas words ordinarily are related to ideas, music is related to the emotions, thus reaching and touching the listener at a vulnerable spot. So it is also with poetry, with literature in many phases, with painting and with sculpture.

The vocabulary of painting is, of course, paints, and that of sculpture marble, granite, clay or plastics. Painting is poetry in color; sculpture is poetry in marble; music is poetry in melody. Each, in its respective category of art, is a morsel of the Infinite revealing itself to man. Each is a translation of life: the poet into verse, the painter into pictures, the sculptor into marble and the musician into song. All speak a language that builds a bridge between the cosmos and the hungering spirit of man.

Whether or not Darwin's hypothesis be true that "the difference between the language of man and the cries of animals is not a difference in kind, but a difference in degree only, a difference of definiteness of connotation and distinctness of articulation," we cannot deny that language is a bridge between humans. It transports my "I" to another and diminishes at least part of the distance that intervenes between us. That which was heretofore *inside* myself ventures *outside* on a mission to reach another, and the rendezvous fulfills that mission. Sometimes it is an intellectual "I" that crosses the bridge, sometimes, as in art and music, it is an aesthetic "I." Sometimes language is used to hide our real thoughts, and even to transmit falsehoods. Every man must determine in his own heart and conscience what standard should govern his commerce with language. A man's character is in a sense related to his use of language, depending on whether language is, as it should be, the servant of his thought, or its master.

Darwin's view of the origin and nature of language, and the investigations conducted by Rousseau in the mid-eighteenth century and by Johann Herder in the third quarter of the same century, cannot be lightly dismissed. But whatever scientific data are available to support their speculations, they in no way refute the majestic statement of Oliver Wendell

Holmes, "Every language is a temple in which the soul of those who speak it is enshrined." This idea seems to support Bergson's evaluation of language in terms of international amity. Said Bergson, "Anyone who is thoroughly familiar with the language and literature of a people cannot be wholly its enemy." Since language grows out of the life, the history and ideals of a people, one familiar with that language will feel closer to its people. If this be true, the stresses in our contemporary world may be considerably mitigated by a concerted effort on the part of nations to learn each other's languages. In so doing they may find a key to the heart of one another.

HERE is a bird known as the halcyon, or kingfisher. It is an unattractive fowl with short tail, broad body and a disproportionately large beak. However, because of its sparkling coat tinged with azure, red ochre and emerald, it ranks among the loveliest tenants in Nature's winged household. In bird lore it is the subject of the following fanciful legend.

"In the beginning of the ages the kingfisher was entirely grey. When it escaped from Noah's Ark it flew off towards the horizon where the sun was sinking. In this flight over the sea to a distant shore, the light of the setting sun clung to its coat, and its breast was dyed for all time with the sun's iridescent rays."

This poetic fancy illustrates a significant psychological principle—the potency of environmental influence. So long as the kingfisher resided in the Ark, flood-bound and hemmed in by a watery prison, its color was a bleak and chilly grey. It reflected the cold hue of its floating dungeon. But once it flew out of the Ark and experienced the magnetic upward pull of beckoning heights, it acquired the dazzling tincture and tone of amber sun and sapphire sky. It seemed to have been magically transformed by its new environment.

Human life, as most psychologists will concede, is likewise influenced by environmental forces. There are some who regard it as being more powerful than heredity. Two and three decades ago, when the nutritional potency of vitamins was recognized, considerable stress was laid on the adage that "we are what we eat." Millennia ago the author of the Book of Proverbs applied this principle to thought life: "As a man thinketh in his heart, so is he." In our modern day psychological and psychoanalytical research have shifted the emphasis to a belief that the ego, carrying a heavy knapsack of suppressions and inhibitions, compels us to be what we are. We are manacled by its chains, with little hope of escape.

But environmental barriers cannot delimit the venturesomeness of the human spirit. Heights and more heights, depths and more depths, are the only horizons it recognizes. Any life concerned only with building an ark to shelter it from storms will be colored with a predominance of grey. Its texture will be drab and uninviting. If we strive, however, to scale the promontoried ledges of our upreaching self, if, like the kingfisher, we soar beyond our earth-bound landmarks, there is no telling what infinitudes we may attain. Every life comprises two selves: an ark-self environed by the body, and a height-self frontiered by the soul. In this dichotomy the latter must dominate the former.

Granted that happiness is a goal all humans devoutly pursue, it is imperative for every individual to arrive at a mature definition of happiness. Perhaps all our definitions will agree upon this common denominator: happiness is not merely an involvement of the senses; it is more than the fruits of merriment and physical satiety. It is something nobler and more durable than pleasure. It derives from unfolding to full expression the spiritual powers implanted within us.

More than nineteen centuries ago Philo made this significant utterance regarding happiness: "It is impossible for man, who is bound up in a mortal body, to be entirely and altogether happy." Whether we concur or dissent, we might agree that happiness, unless freely shared with others, is little more than an "ark" commodity. It must stem from giving as well as from receiving.

Is such a quality of happiness attainable? Yes, if man pursues worthiness as his ultimate objective. The legend of the kingfisher says the flight of the bird was *towards* the sun; it did not reach the sun. We too must set our course towards worthwhile goals. If we link ourselves with selfless causes, the grey within us will be transmuted into a brightness that will shine out of our eyes and out of our hearts. Such a consummation is in itself a source of happiness worth seeking.

For many persons such a source will be wholly inadequate. A Chinese proverb says, "Happiness is like a sunbeam, which the least shadow intercepts, while adversity is often as the rain of spring." It seems incongruous to couple the words "happiness" and "shadow" together, for they represent opposite connotations. But even though they excite contradictory emotions, they meet in a unity that reflects the bitter-sweet of life. If a man does not reach for something higher than his own happiness, he is reaching for a fickle sunbeam that will vanish without leaving a trace.

I cannot leave the subject of happiness without quoting the following anecdote with which Emerson concludes his essay, "The Comic."

"When Carlini was convulsing Naples with laughter, a patient waited on a physician in that city, to obtain some remedy for excessive melancholy, which was rapidly consuming his life. The physician endeavored to cheer his spirits, and advised him to go to the theatre and see Carlini. He replied, 'I am Carlini.'"

HY do men risk life and limb attempting to climb inaccessible mountain ranges? Why should they wish to pit their human strength against these steep and dangerous pyramids of rock and ice and menacing crags? One is appalled by the description of the deadly perils, the well-nigh insuperable obstacles, the ubiquitous imminence of disaster, the dreadful physical suffering and mental anguish due to oxygen deficit, the unsheltered isolation, the haunting desolation, and the dulling of the senses experienced by alpine climbers as they inch their agonizing way across the earth's topmost peaks. Death is their close and constant companion as they mount into sub-zero altitudes. One false step and all is lost. A sudden blizzard and tomorrow will never arrive.

These questions are answered by James Ramsey Ullman in his fascinating book, "Kingdom of Adventure: Everest," which was written before that giant mountain was finally subdued. He points out that mountaineers can no more resist mountain climbing than flowers can refrain from blooming or the heart from beating. They must conquer peaks because they have a climbing mind and a climbing spirit. There is a gravitational pull that urges them upward in somewhat the same manner the law of gravity holds the waters to the earth, attracts them to the moon and governs the planets and stars.

"The men in this book climbed," says Ullman, "because they needed to climb, because that was the way they were made. Lifting their eyes to their mountain, they saw more than rock and ice and snow and the immense emptiness of the sky. They saw, too, a great challenge to their own qualities *as men*; a chance to conquer their own weakness, ignorance and fear; a struggle to match achievement to aspiration and reality to dream. Over and above everything else, the fight for Everest has been an act of faith and affirmation."

What a profoundly perceptive observation we have here! It was expressed at a time when every onslaught on Mount Everest had been turned back by the implacable forces of Nature. It looks beyond the defeats that had strewn the record up to that point; it intimates that man's resoluteness and venturesomeness could not be denied much longer.

That Ullman proved an optimistic prophet is attested by the victory in 1953 of Edmund Hillary and Tensing Norkay who became the first humans to stand on Everest's 29,002 foot summit. This triumph, it will be recalled, electrified the world, and rightly so. But though this was a prodigious feat, its physical implications are not paramount. More important is the fact that man should *want* to stand on the apex of the world's highest mountain. The most significant experience of the human spirit is to dare that which appears beyond man's grasp. There are tasks that seem to mock our human endowments. But over and above those endowments resides an imponderable in man that prompts him to challenge the impossible and to seek the unattainable. We are sculptured out of a sublime pattern that elevates us above physical hurdles.

The *climbing mind* and the *climbing spirit* are our wings. The human soul reaches for heights far beyond the flight of the soaring eagle. The author of Psalm 121 felt the tug of his soul's pinions when he exclaimed, "I lift up mine eyes unto the mountains, from whence shall come my help?" Though he may have fallen again and again, he knew there was within him a song that could not be silenced. It kept chiming, "Ascend, ascend!" One of the Everest climbers expressed a similar thought: "I have often felt the presence of a Companion on the mountains who is not in our earthly party of climbers."

The force that impels men to scale mountains is the same that enabled man to rise above the level of the savage. Man was not created to crawl; he was made to rise. Through the powers of mind and will, of heart and spirit, he hurls defiance at all impediments to his ascent. His upreaching mind and soul are invincible. His battle cry is echoed in "The Ballad of Johnnie Armstrong"—

> I am a little hurt, but I am not slain;
> I will lay me down for to bleed a while,
> Then I'll rise and fight with you again.

Nothing is ever the same
Once it has known the fire;
Whether the furnaced heart
Stoked by coals of desire,
Or kindled fagots of thought
From Truth's white embers caught;
Once it has felt the flame,
Nothing remains the same.

HIS verse was written in a contemplative mood over what is commonly labeled "Man's quest for God." It is a striking phrase, suggesting that in order to find God man need merely institute a search for Him. But this is a fallacy. God is not something that has been lost and needs to be found. Nor is He a faraway hemisphere that must be sought in somewhat the same manner Columbus set out to discover America. Can man's reason or intellect or intuition distil rays powerful enough to penetrate the invisible and the illimitable? It is the same question asked by Job, "Canst thou by searching find God?"

If God may be sought at all, the quest will be successful only if it be directed toward a search for the Good. If we wish to apprehend God we must first become godly, and this can be achieved primarily through the cultivation of goodness. Every human being is a site on which God rears His tabernacle, but the individual must himself supply the foundation materials: righteousness, compassion, forbearance, truthfulness, virtue, and the like. Do not believe the man who says,

"I have searched for God and not found Him." Rather, let him interrogate himself at what point he abdicated the above-mentioned attributes, and for what reasons he bolted the door of his spirit through which God seeks to enter. A human being who successfully labors for the foundation materials of moral rectitude and of sympathy with his fellowman becomes a masterpiece of God. Though fettered by chains of mortality, he merits the seal of the Divine.

When one is fevered with a passionate yearning to attain this seal through a life dedicated to the Good, his questing for God will be more than a random venture. He will understand, even though vaguely, Emerson's reference to God as "the bride or bridegroom of the soul." A Voice will speak within him and refuse to be silenced. It will echo the pronouncement in Deuteronomy, "The Lord thy God is a devouring fire." Jeremiah knew the all-conquering power of that Voice when he cried out, "It was within me as a raging fire shut up in my bosom; I strove to withstand it but I could not." Not until a man's hunger for God's nearness becomes an inner smouldering volcano, will his dark abysses be illumined. He will undergo a complete spiritual transformation. He will become more than he was before, for

> Once he has known the flame
> No one is ever the same.

Finding God is not the result of a searching for Him. It is a personal and immediate experience. It is an awareness of a Companionship paired with the soul. One suddenly discovers embers of Divinity aglow on the hearthstones of his being. God acts on the individual, and the individual reacts with this discovery. His plan is ultimately realized through a partnership between Him and man, the image of Himself. Action and reaction constitute the formula. In philosophy we regard it as cause and effect. Just as vapor ascends to form the cloud, so the glory of God is activated by the impulses that come from man below. In this wise the unsearchable becomes searchable, and man's vision is enlarged by

> Kindled fagots of thought
> From Truth's white embers caught.

Finding God is not an easy undertaking. It means braving the fire to hear His soft footfall on the threshold of our lives. It means risking being singed by the Burning Bush that erupts when He draws near. Finding God means He becomes so real to us that we can hold intimate conversation with him in the manner of Moses as described in Scripture: "And the Lord spoke unto Moses face to face as a man speaketh unto his friend." Perhaps we do not possess the spiritual stature of a Moses, but this should not deter us from *wanting* and *needing* to speak with God face to face.

OME five billion years ago, according to scientists, the universe was not yet in existence. Clouds of gas and dust drifting in space were attracted by the force of gravity to other groups of gas and dust, and merged into larger clouds of matter. These growing clusters began to spin, and when they attained sufficiently high temperatures they became stars. Some broke away and became suns, others planets and comets; one wandered off and became our sun.

A great Cosmic Heart began to throb through the pores of the brooding solitude that encompassed everything. The rhapsody of silence that hymned through whatever space existed, played its last primordial score. A new overtone strained to make its cadence heard. The caverns of chaos were unsealed and the opaque tapestries of darkness were rent asunder. Movement produced action, the stirring of things upon the rim of coming-into-being. Form broke through the hard crust of emptiness and warmth crept out of the convulsive void. Then came life, miraculous, pulsating, incomprehensible life. First it appeared mysteriously in the waters, after two and a half billion years had elapsed. Out of the shadowy beginnings came plant life and soft-bodied single cell creatures. Years passed by in the millions, while life assumed definitive patterns. It breathed into crustaceans, insects, sea scorpions and reptiles; then into fowl and beasts. Finally, as if hungering to reach maturity, it discovered the species that became the ancestor of man.

How puny, how tragically impotent this primitive creature appeared when compared with the sprawling immensities that had witnessed his long, agonizing struggle from beasthood to manhood! And yet, he alone would some day sip the wine of knowledge and taste the nectar of dreams. Though compounded of the same chemicals and minerals found in the red loam, he would become the harp on which the music of a growing civilization was destined to be strummed.

Two master keys were entrusted into his possession: life and death. One was to unlock the portal through which his existence makes its debut; the other was to unbolt the gate leading to the waiting chariot of oblivion.

We shall not speak here of the first key, life; it is the theme of other essays in this collection. But the second key, death, is a profound enigma that thwarts us. Perhaps the mystery will be less bewildering if we can believe with the German philosopher, Johann Fichte: "All death is nature in birth, and at the moment of death appears visibly the rising of life. There is no dying principle in nature, for nature throughout is unmixed life which, concealed beneath the old, begins again and develops itself." If we cultivate such an attitude toward death, should it be hard for us to regard it as notes in an endless aria singing chords of eternity? Why should we fear the summons to nestle some day in the embrace of the Cosmic Heart that set the whole of creation in motion? Why should we cringe in terror before the prospect of ultimately pillowing our weary hearts upon the bosom of eternity? To merge with the sublime harmony that directs and governs the universe, to glide from the harbor of the Here into a shoreless ocean of existence—why should these certainties in a brief uncertain joust with life inspire dread in us?

We betray life if we yield to a fear of death. Because earthly life comprises only a few years, I shall not protest, "It is vain!" Leaves have a briefer existence, yet, how majestically they tiptoe to their autumn doom. They are born; they live; they serve their purpose and die. It is enough for them. It will be enough also for me. I cannot be content with doing less than leaves. I must serve a worthy and useful purpose on the tree of life. I must express the best within me; I must leave behind something worthy of enduring, thus outliving my urn of flesh. When the second master key is placed in my hand, I shall insert it into the lock, pass through the invisible door and fearlessly proceed on my way.

PLOWMAN

OBSERVE a plowman stooped over the kindly brown earth as he sows for the harvest he hopes to reap. There he kneels, in the pose of a worshipper genuflecting in prayer. Hope and faith are his companions as he scatters his seeds, but the bite and lash of a possible rainless season also cast their shadow. Rows of trees standing by the roadside nod their leafy heads like parishioners joining in the worship. For, is not Nature an ally of religion in that she invokes the law of abundant growth and lends her opulence for the fulfillment of the Biblical command, "Be fruitful and multiply"? It was Emerson who remarked, "What is a farm but a mute gospel." From the advent of spring, when the first furrow leans against the soil, through summer and autumn, sun and rain, wheat and chaff, weeds and fruits, blight and birth—all bear witness to Nature's testament.

This knowledge is not alien to the farmer I am describing. A few weeks earlier he had completed his plowing chore. His task was wearying, but not lacking in exhilaration. His plow was a creative quill inscribing the theme of palpitant growth on the dark parchment beneath him. He has long learned that labor on the soil is God's pedagogy. The seeds he sows are pregnant with the life impulse which will anoint the earth and draw infant grain out of her womb. The land is his, and he belongs to the land—it is home to him. Roots and stems and branches are his great library. How to make them grow productively is the goal of his education.

With this in mind, he surveys his earth-palace. Day and night, in rain and in drouth, with and without sun, the earth must work for him and yield crops. Bolts of thunder roaring hoarsely on a frowning day, streaks of lightning piercing the clouds to empty their storehouse of needed water, cooling winds upon carpets of dew—these are his allies, his friends. He is not alone in the conquest of the land. The glow of expectancy in his breast is not unlike the flaming taper borne by a priest to the sacrarium in his mosaic-domed cathedral. The sower and the priest use different tools; each comes with his particular hoe. But both are plowmen in God's field. One strengthens earth's miraculous brotherhood by coaxing throbbing, benevolent life out of her swollen veins. The other enhances human brotherhood by plowing in man's spirit a furrow that will fructify with the grain of godliness. One resorts to tillage that will produce bread; the other to cultivation that will blossom better souls. Both must be patient; the one waiting for unhurrying Nature to perform her task slowly with chemicals and minerals, the other patiently tolerant of man's callousness and obduracy that resist and retard the progress of spiritual sowing.

Perhaps all of us should regard ourselves as sowers in life's unplowed field. Hopefully we till the soil of our needs and longings in anticipation of a rich yield. With trembling hands we knock at the doors of our human nature and stretch out our arms for a goodly share of gifts. Often we forget that seeds must be deposited before a harvest becomes possible. For whatever seeds we actually plant, we expect a hundredfold in return. We want each seed to burgeon into a generous future store. We will rankle with discontentment if our sowing is not rewarded with affluence. We demand compensation for whatever labors we contribute; we evaluate theology in terms of recompense.

In appraising life, this bitter axiom seems to be fundamental in human experience: there are many sowers, but not many who gather an abundant harvest. How many succeed in hurdling the numerous barricades that obstruct the road to plenitude? All bend down to gather sheaves, but multitudes rise up empty handed. Their hopes are infirm scaffolds from which splintered aspirations dangle like grotesque scarecrows. The frenetic tone of life's *Nay* harmonizes with their melancholy theme of adversity. They look to their inner orchards but find them heavy with barrenness. There are not sufficient ripened ears to fill the granary of their yearnings. Nature's sceptre was not held out for them.

Shall man then cease sowing because he is often denied the fruits of his labors? Surely, this cannot be the answer. The task, O sower, is to implant seeds even though others may gather the harvest. Plow and plowman, like body and soul, must unite in a covenant to enrich mankind, be the contribution ever so little. Life's sanctification begins with sowing, not with reaping. Planting is the act of worship; harvesting is the Amen. Sowers are God's ministers, often lonely and ignored, who plant seeds of the spirit because this is their votive offering to life. They are not necessarily concerned with reaping; they are unencumbered by the disappointments and frustrations others experience from lack of gathering. Like the farmer who conquers himself when he seeks to exercise dominion over his field, the sower knows he is not without wealth even though the crops he made possible become the wealth of many who do not sow. He may not have heaped fodder into his private warehouse, but he finds ample reward in knowing he has brought greater gleanings to mankind.

ITHDRAW occasionally for a few moments from things prosaic and gaze into heaven's irradiant nocturnal span. In that celestial meadow you will behold millions of spangled forget-me-nots blooming in the grotto of night. Clusters of nebulae will waltz before you, and the vastness of the interstellar spaces will fill you with awe. You will undoubtedly be constrained to ask the questions uttered by a sensitive poet, "What are ye orbs? The words of God? The Scriptures of the skies?"

When I contemplate my paltry years I am poignantly conscious of the brief span of human life. Time means no more than the watch on my left wrist. But in the presence of the stars I am aware of the existence of light-years, and both time and space become more meaningful to me. I stand in wonderment before the encircling distances that extend from star to star, from planet to planet. I marvel at the incredible harmony and symmetry that govern these denizens prowling through the black abyss of night. To be able to feast my eyes upon all this celestial grandeur, to embark upon an imaginary breathtaking tour of this cosmic wonderland, to ponder the mystery that begems the upper chambers with emeralds and opals and blazing sapphires—how can I compare my earthly crumbs with such an incalculable hoard? I feel closer to the great Architect who kindled the first fires of Creation and guided these stars in their rhythmic migrations. I am reminded of Carlyle's soliloquy: "When I gaze into the stars, they look down upon me with pity from their serene and silent places, like eyes glistening with tears over the little lot of man."

One cannot commune with the stars without feeling a sense of deep humility. The bigness of the stellar universe emphasizes the insignificance of our own tiny planet as well as the littleness of mortal man. This is a salutary reaction. When we look at the image of ourselves in a mirror, we are often prone to become complacent, uncritical, haughty, overweening with self-importance. Our thoughts fly towards the tinsel-goals that preoccupy us, like moths winging aimlessly towards a wisp of light. But when our gaze mounts the lofty podium of the tranquil stars, we cannot help feeling we are looking into the mirror of God. Something of soul dominates the consciousness of flesh. We sense an inscrutable kinship between the infinite heavens and our infinite soul. Both wear the same mantle of timelessness. Both are gleaming ornaments in the treasure-trove of eternity.

Becoming acquainted with the stars inspires in us the habit of trying to stand on tiptoe. The dust-in-us recedes as we seek to find a fitting environment for our height-hungry spirit. Thus elevated, we learn a lesson humanity needs desperately to learn in these days of atomic peril. The primer of the skies instructs us how we humans might emulate the activity of stars, which have existed since time crept out of its hazy chrysalis.

The chief lesson is that the stars occupy their far-flung empires in perfect harmony. They have never warred against one another; they have never sought to extinguish each other's orb of light. They have never scarred the beauty of the heavens; on the contrary, they have enhanced their majesty.

Man, on the other hand, has inhabited the earth only a few thousand years, and see how frequently and with what savagery he has marred its loveliness! He has drenched its fruitful fields with the blood of his brother. He has pocked its hills and valleys with desolation of internecine conflict. He has cluttered it with ugly slums. Above him is the illimitable dominion of stars, but within him lurks the serpent of avarice that seeks profit from every acre of ground. The music of the spheres psalms in the skies, but he pays more attention to the thud of his own lumbering feet running for gain.

Let man pause in his headlong rush for material things and ponder the secrets revealed by the stars. Let him cease substituting the image of his puny self for the wider realities his life must pursue. Let him decipher the speech of the stars and he will better understand the speech of his own winged spirit.

OME years ago it was my happy privilege to be in the audience when the late Arturo Toscanini conducted the NBC Symphony Orchestra in a program of enchanting music. For well-nigh two hours I felt transported as if on wings. It was a memorable experience surcharged with a fervor I distinctly recall as I write these lines, and again I have an awareness of the rhythm, meter and melody that soothed my inner agitations. Perhaps it is true that music, through which soul speaks to soul, is prayer at its highest level. Musical notes frequently strike an incandescence far brighter than candles burning on a church altar.

As I watched Toscanini, he seemed intent on extracting not only the intonations and overtones, but also the color and shape of the notes emerging from the instruments massed in the semicircle before him. He appeared to be translating a manuscript written in a universal language. I could not be certain whether other-worldly vibrations were pouring into him from some mysterious source, or whether hidden adagios were being extracted out of his deepest self. But of the truth of this conclusion there could be no doubt at all: "Music is the fourth great material want of our nature—first food, then raiment, then shelter, then music." There are doors within us that can be opened only through music.

Several months later I contemplated a circumstance that had originally excited merely my passing curiosity. I refer to the "tuning up" process that always takes place as a preliminary to a symphony concert. Before Toscanini made his appearance, many of the musicians proceeded to strike tentative notes on their respective instruments. For some minutes there was a continuous babel of sound: here the thrumming of violins and cellos and the fingering of harps, there shrill clusters of notes on flutes and piccolos; now the reedy tones of oboes, and again chords from trumpets and horns. . . By the time Toscanini ascended the podium, each instrument had been individually tuned; and when he raised his baton as a signal to begin, the musicians were ready for the harmonic unity the symphony was intended to achieve. Their first requirement was to be in tune.

This need to be in tune runs like a golden thread throughout life's rhapsody no less than through a superbly trained orchestra. Two elements are involved. First, the individual instrument must be tested for accuracy of tone and pitch; this may be termed "tuning up." Secondly, each instrument must fulfil its particular function in harmony with the other instruments participating in the musical work; this may be denominated "tuning with." This duality is indispensable. Each instrument is its own little world, charged with a unique mission. But the *summum bonum* is attained only when each individual instrument helps to create the larger world symbolized by the symphony.

Human life is subject to this same pattern. It must engage in the dual project of "tuning up" and "tuning with." Every person as an individual is entitled to full development according to his special personal needs and aspirations. Nothing should interfere with his quest for wholeness and with his yearning to achieve his destiny. Heine correctly observed: "Every single man is a world which is born and which dies with him; beneath every gravestone lies a world's history."

And yet, while the individual person is the cornerstone of democracy and of civilization itself, he cannot overlook his duty to society. He owes an obligation to the group, and however successful he has been in integrating his personality, he is a gross failure if he does not contribute something to the strengthening of the group of which he is an inseparable part. A life is incomplete that does not attune itself with society.

There is another direction in which this dual project may be pointed. We are subject to two distinct and separate wills: our own, which is human, and God's, which is Divine. The former stems from ourselves and communicates itself through the intelligence; the latter is both transcendent and immanent, and addresses us through a suprasensual perceptiveness known as intuition. Our own will must be periodically scrutinized, to make certain it is tuned up for life's worthwhile undertakings. At the same time, we must be tuned with the eternal inflow which courses into our spirit from God's tides.

With what higher Symphony do we strive to harmonize our lives? Through our physical, psychic and intellectual faculties we create a blueprint that develops our ego to full stature. But there is another unity with which we must merge our ego—a oneness with Divinity. He who learns thus to attune himself becomes conversant with an orchestration that echoes the transfiguring music of Deity.

SEED VERSUS ROCK

LACE a seed next to a rock and the contrast becomes amazingly onesided. The great rock dwarfs the seed in size, in weight, in density and in sheer elemental strength. To attempt a comparison through the perceptive sense would seem utter folly. The solid rock juts out like a stupendous giant, the very acme of power, stability and permanency. The seed appears so fragile, so delicate; it can easily be crushed between the fingers of a child. But pit the seed against the massive boulder, and a prodigious contest takes place between them. When the combat commences, it seems inevitable that the rock must triumph over the seed. What chance has a midget David against the colossal Goliath?

But after a period of years the seed conquers the rock. Its height-hungry tendrils probe unceasingly along the surface and sides of the rock, seeking a vulnerable spot before launching its offensive that will not be denied. Spurred by the mystery of life imprisoned within it, the seed dispatches bold patrols into every defiant crevice, and once a foothold is gained, the ultimate result can no longer be in doubt. Its germinating vitality is no match for the inanimate boulder. Its greedy roots claw at the defenseless skin of the granite ledge and carve their brown autograph into fissures against which centuries of hurricanes, whirlwinds and icy tempests have lashed in vain. Silently, insistently, it deposits its life-germ into every aperture, into every cleft and rift, until a bridge-head is firmly established.

Years speed by on the tracks of time. Springs, summers, autumns and winters leave their calling cards and travel on.

The rootlets expand; they stretch their arms and spread deeper and ever deeper into the grudgingly yielding flint. The irrepressible law of vitality, ordained and enacted in the parliament of God, has broken down all opposition. It has won a superb triumph.

Here we have a parable of history, of life itself. The law of vitality, the affirmation of life, is a divine mandate. It is the seal of durability, the invincible germ of creativity which presses forward into fullness of realization. Size alone is no criterion. Bigness devoid of vitality is no passport to permanency. Smallness saturated with vitality contains the self-revelation of the Creator, and is therefore destined to endure.

Religion affirms the same statute as does the conquest of seed over rock. Man's progress is the story of the spirit vanquishing the rock of materialism. Something within man, nurtured by the same vitality that enabled the delicate seed to master the coarse rock, infuses his life with a germ of eternity. The unyielding crag of mortality holds no terror for his soul's potentialities. He mounts above the seen into the circumambient unseen, and explores inner trails that lead to a highway higher than himself. He senses intuitively a Presence that is within his life and yet above it. Somewhere, in pinnacles of himself that beckon upward, he receives an answer of height calling unto height and deep unto deep. Out of this ineffable experience comes the blossoming seed of the spirit into faith. No rock, however flinty, can stand before such a faith. It conquers all.

Religion is the seed out of which burgeon blooms of abiding worth. Man, with starshine in his eyes, scans the heightward road and follows it until he sees the footprints of the Divine within the focus of his vision. He splinters the rock of finiteness and plants in its ruins the seed of life indestructible. Intimations of Infinitude expand his physical horizons. His existence is no longer a sum of fragments called years; it is a deathless link in the wide-engirdling existence of the All. It bursts upon him in a triumphant refrain, and as he takes up the chorus he learns how he

> Can crowd eternity into an hour,
> Or stretch an hour into eternity.

LMOST every person is impelled to cry out at some crucial period in life, "Why is God silent when I need Him so desperately?" Frequently, when our hearts quaver under a crushing burden of wretchedness, a baffling silence tends to exacerbate the unutterable woe that torments us. We ask questions, but there seems to be no answer. We look for help, but it appears we are alone. We repeat the plaint of Isaiah, "Verily Thou art a God who hidest Thy face." We hunger for some tiny token of Divine assurance, but like an eternal Sphinx He chooses not to speak.

How shall we account for such an austere silence in our hours of need? Certainly, it cannot be that God is so preoccupied with His own omnipotence that He does not concern Himself with the grimacing pain carved upon our finite features. We believe He is an immanent, omnipresent Deity who "comes to us without bell." It is unthinkable that barriers can be set up between God the Creator and man the created. Our souls are corridors through which His indwelling Presence enters our being and His overbrimming radiance makes contact with our consciousness. How, then, shall we account for His silence?

If God's communications do not reach us, it does not follow that He is deaf to human cries. As man acts, God reacts; if there be no Divine reaction, it may well be due to the character of man's action. Isaiah's reference to the "hidden God" of the physical universe does not deny His revelation in our moral life. No supplication ever goes unanswered. Sometimes the answer is Yes, sometimes No, and sometimes

Wait. But man is too impatient to wait. He wants his answer immediately.

If our cry to God is merely an act of the lips and tongue, how can we expect *not* to be greeted with an inscrutable stillness. Communion with God can be established only through the combined interplay of the heart and mind, of the soul and will. A call which represents an act of the deepest spirit will never fail to evoke a response. It is far removed from the plane of mumbling monologue which is little more than a soliloquy. It becomes an authentic dialogue between ourselves and God. We no longer feel like a desolate wilderness swept by scorching sands of sorrow and hurt. Rather, we feel like a child nestling unafraid upon the warm bosom of its mother.

Many face a great silence when they call upon God because they are silent whenever God calls upon them. We are slow to realize that God is always calling upon us, always striving to break through the material walls that close us in. But we go about our mundane ways without giving heed. We rely completely upon our own human vocabulary, only to discover some day that it is inadequate for speech with the Divine. One must be conversant with a Divine vocabulary in order to converse with the Divine.

They who do not cultivate such a vocabulary through their moral faculties, fail to perceive the music of His fellowship. They become estranged from the Divine idiom for which there can be no outside interpreter. They believe it is God's silence casting shadows across the barren cliffs of their great need. But they are in error. *It is their own silence to God that has come back to haunt them.* They are like the builders of the Tower of Babel whose language became confounded. They will remain thus confounded until they learn this simple theorem of the spirit: He who does not learn how to answer when God calls, will not possess the spiritual password when he himself finds it necessary to call.

God's silence—there is no such thing! He speaks to every individual attuned to His revelations. Whatever silence exists is in man himself. It stems from his failure to subordinate his will to the Divine will and to become familiar with a spiritual vocabulary God speaks. His emptiness is unfilled because he has nothing to give to God. Let him utter prayers that cry out of his spirit, and a Divine reply will come to him like a benediction shining through the gloom of his heartache.

UMAN nature is a Dr. Jekyl and Mr. Hyde. Like the idol Janus, facing east and west at the same time, human nature frequently is two-faced. The instincts, emotions, sensations, impulses and predilections crowded into the crypts of human nature, play dual roles that are sometimes difficult to reconcile. Consciousness of its own volition knows neither the law of restraint nor the pattern of discipline. The congenital aspect of the human makeup is wild and uninhibited. It undergoes modification and training only through the influence of forces imposed from without. The raw materials of our moral heritage are like an unplanted seed. They do not fructify unless they are carefully and properly husbanded.

Happily, the birthright of a modern child comes into an environment of civilization. But this does not mean the child is born a civilized being. On the contrary, if you leave the child to its own instincts it will grow into behavior patterns that will differ little, if at all, from the primitive patterns of a child in an uncivilized milieu. Human nature, when left completely to its own devices, recognizes only the authority of evolution. Untamed impulses have to be bred out in order to fit the child for a place in society. The animal within must be trained to suppress the primordial drives that are basic to uncultivated human nature.

Training is the principal, indeed the indispensable, function of civilization. It must prepare man, whose primal equipment includes the law of tooth and claw, to accept a corpus of social and moral legislation. It must widen man's distance from beasthood and help him gain mastery over the inborn predispositions that served him during earlier periods in his evolution.

From this standpoint, we can readily understand and account for the unremitting conflict within human nature. Did not the Biblical author admonish millennia ago, "The imagination of man's heart is evil from his youth"? Even when effectively saddled, the primitive animal is always with us. The drives that goad man on are nature made; the controls that inhibit him are self made. Religion, ethics, moral suasion, have been perennially invoked to weight the scales in favor of self-discipline. But the tug of war is never terminated. The inner beast is never completely quiescent.

This explains, at least in some measure, the puzzling ambivalence of human nature. It helps us understand the paradox of man possessing the capacity to love and to hate, to be merciful and ruthless, to be liberal and fanatical, to exercise tenderness and to give vent to barbaric passions. He is at the same time humble and ambitious, peaceful and militant, creative and destructive, an altruist and an egotist, a paragon of humaneness towards friends and a ferocious tiger against enemies. He is an angel and a devil, generous and covetous, cooperative and self-aggrandizing. At times he manifests an exquisite trait of brotherhood, at others he sinks to the nadir of prejudice. No wonder Heine referred to men as "the other kind of livestock." One who is half angel and half brute must always witness and experience inner warfare.

If these observations appear to be exaggerated, let me quote a statement by Sir Arthur Keith, one of the world's outstanding anthropologists. Said he, "In the world of humanity there are only savages, who differ in the degree to which they have masked their original nature in the cloak of civilization." Evolution patterned man's nature for tribal life; civilization detribalizes him. Herein lies the cause of his conflict. The voice of his nearest congeners, the gorilla and chimpanzee, sometimes breaks through the curtains of time, and there is a recrudescence of the ape in man.

But a new man will some day emerge. Though the veneer of his civilization is often only skin deep, we may hope confidently that man will become the master, rather than the slave, of his dual nature. I feel with Emerson that man is the channel through which heaven flows to earth. He has demonstrated the genius to tame many phases of Nature, and will utilize the same genius to extract the noblest and the best out of his own nature.

T THE age of twenty-three Thomas Wolfe
wrote a biographical essay entitled, "God's Lonely Man." It
was a reaction to his belief that life had saddled him with a
disproportionate share of loneliness. When he grew older,
however, he changed the title, not because he was displeased
with it, but because he realized loneliness is a normal and
inescapable condition of human existence. The passing years
taught him it is salutary to explore the hidden labyrinths of
one's being and drink nourishment from the fountains of
solitude. It is good to roam alone with one's soul, in keeping
with Byron's remark, "In solitude we are least alone," and
with Thoreau's confession, "I never found the companion
that was so companionable as solitude."

Psychologists seldom differ about the potency and uni-
versality of the gregarious instinct. In human beings, no less
than in animals, there is an irresistible impulse to herd together. A common yearning for mutual protection and companionship possesses all living creatures. Thackeray gave voice
to this yearning in his plaint, "How lonely we are in the
world! You and I are but a pair of isolations, with some
fellow islands a little more or less near to us."

To be alone seems contrary to the laws both of Nature
and of human nature. Human beings gravitate toward the
crowd. The group brings the individual a sense of vicarious
solidarity. Aloneness serves to heighten a feeling of isolation.
Alone, one becomes a prey to wind and storm, to fears and
doubts. But merged with the group, he leans upon the cumu-

lative strength of numbers, and thereby finds greater power in himself.

There are, however, stoical and resolute souls who learn how to convert aloneness into an asset. De Quincey learned it: "Solitude, though it may be silent as light, is, like light, the mightiest of agencies; for solitude is essential to man." An exacting self-discipline is required to create such an asset, but once achieved its rewards enrich the spirit. Ibsen touched upon this truth when he remarked, "The strongest man in the world is he who stands most alone." Lincoln's life demonstrated this truth.

He who must always lose himself in the company of others seldom if ever tastes the wine that flows out of the vineyard of his inmost being. He remains a stranger to his pristine self. There are times when aloneness must be embraced like a bride. How else can we penetrate into the private and intimate chambers where we may divest ourselves of all inhibitions and artificialities? How else can we court the creative ideas and ideals that are wooed when we are most alone with ourselves? One who becomes "God's Lonely Man" in this sense, is the recipient of a permanent benediction. It is a fructifying seed; it blossoms into a spiritual orchard one can never find in a crowd.

I do not advocate withdrawal from the active and challenging pursuits of daily living. Nor do I espouse a hermit-like privacy. I merely point out there are times when we must be alone with our own soul, with our own thoughts and dreams. We must learn the art of making use of solitude. The hushed sessions with ourselves may well be far more eloquent than the raucous hubbub of the milling crowd. We rely too much upon life's stridencies and too little upon meditation. We defraud ourselves of divine experiences when we remain alien to the solitary altars hidden in our own deeps. The oratorios chorusing from these altars cannot be matched by the popular melodies hummed by the regimented group.

If we pause long enough to recline under the shade-tree of our spirit, we shall suddenly discover the deeper roots to which we are tied. We will hear songs that are never heard on congested highways. Perhaps we shall occasionally become aware that the crowd is far away, but we shall not feel lonely. We shall better understand Swift's significant words, "He is never less alone than when he is alone."

YOU are asked, "What time is it?" You glance at your watch, note the position of the two hands, and calculate the hour. But is this really telling time?

Strictly speaking, we do not tell time at all. Reading the dial on a clock creates only an illusory interpretation of time. It involves only a mechanical process. Since the dawn of civilization, men have agreed upon some common artificial pattern to express the time element in their human intercourse. The sun dial, the hour glass, the clock and calendar, are the mind's visible instruments to spy upon a whirling tide of eternity that transcends the mind's farthermost outposts. In reality, it is all a mirage.

When we say it is eight o'clock in the morning, or eight o'clock in the evening, we are merely describing the position of our planet in relation to the sun at that given moment. "Morning" and "evening" are words that compute the space intervening between the sun and ourselves, nothing more. If proof be needed for this concept, we find it in the fact that while it is morning in one part of the world it is evening in some other hemisphere.

Whatever moment comes into our ken, our consciousness reaches out to grasp it. We cannot, however, hold on to it, for in seizing it we knell its end, and it vanishes like a heartbeat that has done its work. The birth of a moment is its passport to death. How and whence it came, and whither it goes, from what concealed path it entered and through what gateway it makes its exit, are mysteries too profound for the human intellect to unravel. Perhaps the word "change" would be a more accurate synonym for what we now call time.

Time is not a matter of clocks or of calendars. It is a *quality* rather than a *quantity*. Its measure is neither mechanical nor physical. It emerges from a cosmic flow which, in the physical realm, is comparable to invisible springs pushing their waters through the veins of the earth. We live in time, not time in us. We cease to live when time, becoming frozen, changes to molten death. The fragments of infinity temporarily entrusted into our care withdraw from us, and that which we called our lifetime is ended. But every moment is a complete lifetime in itself. Every hour is a unit of timelessness. Every year is a courier from the flood of eternity that bathes the shores of our existence. We are part of that eternity and that eternity is part of us.

The mind is too restricted a vessel to apprehend eternity, much less to define it. But why even attempt to define the undefinable? It should be sufficient for us to recognize that every moment of our lives is dipped in eternity. Through the windows of the spirit we catch an occasional evanescent glimpse of its horizonless vista. The world itself may be a chimera, only a mask to clothe the things with which our lives come in contact. But eternity, even though beyond our power to define, is the reality that gives stature to time.

Now, what is eternity? Certainly not a mortgage on the future. Eternity is now—this breath we draw, this heartbeat throbbing within us, this hope we cherish, this song we sing, this hurt we feel, this beauty we behold, this falsehood that deludes us, this truth we affirm. . . . Time is merely the shadow of eternity, the now through whose lens we gaze beyond today. It is the substance we knead and mold into a pathway towards Infinitude.

Time breaks off at some point in our lives, but eternity goes on and takes our spiritual ego with it. Therefore, though we are concerned with watches and calendars, with days and months and years, though we shall surrender our physical space on this planet, we are companioned by an unconquerable immortality that will embrace us the moment we cease to commute in time's rickety coach. Then, if one should ask, "What time is it?" we shall answer, "It is eternity."

ROM the time man first became aware of his power of comprehension, he has striven mightily to break loose from his earthfooted moorings. He has always been the perennial seeker, eager to rise above the vast loneliness of his desert heritage. Numerous and diverse have been the goals to which he hitched the chariot of his aspirations. With hungry, questioning eyes he scanned the trodden path of his wanderings, determined to fathom the meaning of the shadow of himself etched upon everything his feet touched. He yearned to sunder the dark veils that intervened between himself and the phenomena his vague understanding could not penetrate. There were times when he cringed from life as though it were a menacing javelin hurled by some malevolent hand.

One day he grew conscious of a sensation he had never experienced before. Something within him stirred ever so tremulously, and he was filled with a curious restlessness to apprehend its meaning. It was the first time something incorporeal, a spiritual phase of himself, stepped forth and challenged him face to face. Until that moment he had been a creature of fear, lashed by invisible whips that terrified him. Now new thoughts walked across the threshold of his thinking; like priests marching with lighted candles, new ideas entered the fane of his mind. The shadow of himself no longer affrighted him; he had been beguiled into fleeing from it as from an enemy. The manifestations of Nature would no longer send him hurtling into headlong flight. He began to seek explanations for the reason of things that had completely mystified him in the past. In short, he initiated the practice of using his brain no less than his emotional arsenal.

Thenceforth his curiosity and inquisitiveness became his allies and instilled in him a sense of defiance. Instead of fleeing from thunder and lightning, he stood his ground and pelted them with stones and arrowheads. No longer cringing before the elements, he dared believe he might tame them. The purple mountains, humping their mammoth shoulders into the vault of space, were no longer jungle lairs for snarling evil spirits. Their heights were the shadow of heights he dimly began to feel rising in himself. Their dreams were part of his own brooding, and the storms that lashed their peaks were outer manifestations of the agitations that welled in his own heart. At long last, he had grown out of his cocoon of infancy.

Man has come a long way since those early days. But one characteristic remains unchanged: he has never ceased to be the perennial seeker.

Legion are the things man's searching mind has scrutinized, and many are the secrets he has lured from the earth beneath his feet and from the universe above, around and within him. Athirst for knowledge, he has unlocked doors once considered forever bolted to human inquiry. He has solved many of Nature's profoundest riddles, and has translated his discoveries into benevolent patterns that have greatly enhanced life. Although still earthfooted, he soars through the stratosphere at speeds that defy gravity, and he plunges into oceans with steel leviathans that laugh at depths and storms. He sits in New York and speaks to Bombay in India. He stands in front of the 200-inch Palomar telescope and glimpses galaxies that have been traveling towards us for millions of years. The perennial seeker has indubitably become the great finder.

But one quest remains incomplete—man's search for himself. Despite the progress achieved by sociology, psychology and psychiatry, man has not yet reached the gateway to self-realization and self-fulfillment. The human problem still eludes solution. There are too many hollow lives in our contemporary world. There is too much emptiness and too little creativity among the great majority of our world population. Anxiety, neuroticism, despair and escapism are unsurmounted walls the human mind has not yet broken down. So long as men are content merely to be, the goal of their search will never be attained. Only when they strive consciously to become more than they are, will men discover the key that will open the untapped treasure house of their human potentials.

CCORDING to an ancient myth, there is an image asleep in a block of marble until it is awakened by the sculptor. The sculptor must himself feel that he is not so much inventing or shaping the curve of breast or shoulder but is delivering the image from its prison.

When Phidias, the designer of the imposing Parthenon, created the statue of his enormous Olympian Zeus, he must have felt he was releasing a god from marble. When Michelangelo stood before the massive slabs out of which his young David and the austere Moses were to be shaped, his role was greater than that of mere sculptor. His task was to release the forms that lay interred in those marble tombs. He was to refashion two personalities into a pattern beyond the power of the grave to lay away.

The mammoth blocks that had been wrenched out of the earth's deep quarries were made to disgorge the contour and life, the power and rugged beauty that were potential in their inchoate mold. Immortality was snatched out of their frozen embrace. With heart and perceptiveness, with hammer and chisel, Michelangelo shattered the walls of limbo time had thrown around these conspicuous figures in the Old Testament. Centuries were bridged, and the past recaptured. It is reported that when Michelangelo had completed his Moses, he struck it sharply with his hammer and bade it to speak, even as Moses had struck the lifeless rock at Horeb and commanded it to pour forth living waters. So perfectly had the lips been chiseled that they appeared tremulous with speech.

The influence wielded by the sculptor on his materials

comforms to an all-embracing law extending into every category of being, great and small, animate and inanimate. From the law of gravity down to the tender gaze of a mother evoking a smile in her infant, we behold its omnipresence. The heaving tides are the sculpture formed by the attraction of moon and sun. The distant stars exert a benedictive attraction upon the timid flower in its lowly garden alcove. Spring and autumn, summer and winter, are carved into being by the position of the sun's center across the Equator. Water is magically drawn to depressions in the earth's surface, and as a result, interlaceries of lakes spread their liquid statuary beneath the enamoured sky. The law of influence is, indeed, a cosmic mandate.

Let us consider now the possibilities of human sculpture. If resistant marble can be made to liberate images, if truth can be kindled into a fire by the poet, if the jungle beast can be stripped of its ferocity by the animal trainer, if a George Washington Carver and a Luther Burbank can coax the soil to yield products Nature herself did not plan, what grandeur must be yearning to be freed in man! What marvelous fruits must be waiting to burgeon out of the loam of his being! Shaped by salutary influences, he has the potential to rise to undreamed-of heights. To what mountain peaks of greatness he may ascend if he will but surrender himself completely to the spiritual influences that chisel dust into Divinity! If marble and beast, lacking the gifts of mind and spirit, can be made to advance from lower to higher status, one can only speculate how high and how far man will advance if he will but develop his latent potentialities.

Every individual is a sculptor, and his first subject is self. There is a Divinity waiting to be liberated within every personality. With tools of heart and brain and spirit we must hew the hard granite of our nature into loftier patterns. But this is not our sole task as rational beings. We must also touch the lives of those around us and contribute to their lives something worthwhile in ourselves. We must strive to make human statuary more noble, more sublime. We must help to carve away the chaos and darkness that hold mankind in bondage. The whole of humanity must participate in this sculpturing mutuality. It is possible to draw out of ourselves and out of our fellowman the same positive expression Michelangelo drew out of granite and Toscanini out of Haydn's Largo of the G Major Symphony. We cannot, of course, ever hope to parallel the works of these masters, but this limitation does not relieve us of our responsibility to make at least a minor contribution to the enhancement of human sculpture.

CLOSE YOUR EYES AND SEE

PHILOSOPHER once counseled, "If you wish to see, close your eyes." If taken literally, such a procedure would insure not-seeing rather than seeing. How, one might ask, can the sense of sight be exercised through closed eyes? It sounds like sheer effrontery for Plotinus to have remarked, "The knowledge of the senses is truly ludicrous." But he was referring to thoughts of the heart as contradistinguished from thoughts of the brain. An insight within man reveals far more than his eyes can tell him. It is an oracular perception that discloses secrets before they are discovered by the sensory organs. It is like catching a haunting melody that has always been humming in the soul. It outruns logic; it *knows* even before the knowledge has cast its shadow. It receives enlightening intimations from a special Wisdom that freely showers its hospitality. Our understanding may not immediately grasp its activity, since it is a presentiment rather than an experience.

This idea harmonizes with the philosophy of Immanuel Kant. According to the skeptical philosophy of John Locke, whatever makes its way to the intellect must do so by the previous experience of the senses. Kant dissented. Reversing Locke's hypothesis, he pointed out "that there was a very important class of ideas or imperative forms which did not come by experience, but through which experience was acquired." These intuitions not only precede experience, but actually control it. There are things we share first, then see afterwards. We sit at the feet of an inexplicable intelligence whose pedagogy affects us through our involuntary perceptions. Its tutelage makes us the recipients of a lore that reaches us spontaneously. The mind seeks to analyze that lore later, if at all.

"If you wish to see, close your eyes." So preoccupied are we with mathematical lines that intervene between our vision and the external objects it espies, that we are blind to the lights and shadows, to the arcs and curves, and to the ivied walls of the university housed within us. We gaze with awe at the blue-gold clusters of stars that bloom in the vineyard of the heavens, and so we should. But there is greater awe in the realization that planets and heavens, orbs of dawn and beams of twilight, height and breadth, are not accessible merely to our eyes; they are also in the unfathomable deeps within us. The harsh, impersonal external world obstructs our view of them.

The Great White Way, Orion and Arcturus, Sirius and the Pleiades, all roam through the shoreless spaces. But they also chart their course in the firmament that horizons our hearts. If this seems mysterious or esoteric, it is because we stare with bewildered eyes upward, and seldom with contemplative eyes downward through the conduits of perception that brings us to the soul's floor.

The world of space and time is never still, but in constant flux. As it whirls in unceasing transit around us, we catch fugitive glimpses of its outer layers. This world of time and space is, however, not the sole universe in which we live and have our being. We wander through canyons and scale cliffs the eye cannot perceive. Close your eyes and meditate amid a breath of quietude, surrender for a few moments to the embrace of solitude, and you will see the outlines of an overworld which is the Source of the rivulet that is your life. Be still and ponder, and you will envision the spires of timelessness that rise within you. You will become aware of a dimension that will enable you, as if illumined by a sudden streak of lightning, to apprehend the soul's immediate vision. The eye of the flesh will not descry it. The abysses of the body are too deep for the physical eye to penetrate. But if, during your quiet concentration, you will have enough stamina to bypass these abysses and march on alone, you will see a Companion and feel a Companionship approaching from immensities you did not know you possessed.

The title of Paul Claudel's *The Eye Listens,* bears a relationship to the theme of this essay. The fly-leaf announces, "Through the magic of his pen great painters like Vermeer van Delft, Rembrandt, Frans Hals, Goya, Velasquez, Rubens, Titian and many others are not only made visible in their works, but are—through a subtle process of the mind—*brought to all the senses of the human soul.*"

The italicized words furnish a clue for the understanding of the intriguing title, *The Eye Listens.* The word "senses" certainly extends beyond the traditional connotation of that term. The eye does not listen with the organ of hearing. When it gazes at a sunset emptying decanters of roses upon a hushed mountainside, it hears far more than it sees. When it spies a timid leaf falling in autumn from weary branches, it hears the lullaby of Mother earth calling to her own. When it looks upon the telltale furrows suffering has plowed upon a human face, it not only hears the melancholy cries perhaps long stifled, but actually feels the hurt. The "third eye" is more than an instrument of seeing; it possesses the faculty also of hearing.

Close your eyes and see! The unseen can be apprehended only through the optics of the spirit. Too many of us permit closed doors to conceal the ineffable light of the soul. Beyond the clamor of our diurnal struggle, beyond our fretting and fearing, there are frontiers we never reach. Gaze at them through the soul's wide-open window and you will experience the beatific intuition of dawns gleaming within you and stars nestling in your heart.

HAT prompts a bird to sing? One obvious answer is that a bird's song is its medium of articulation, its uttered vocabulary. Another answer is that the contact of curved wings with arching heights gives birth to silver notes which are the living progeny of melody. The resultant chansons are the mating of heights betrothed to pinions. Perhaps this is the cryptic meaning concealed in the Biblical verse, "A bird of the air shall carry the voice, and that which hath wings shall tell the matter."

The song of a bird is not merely a cluster of notes cascading into a tuneful strain. It is part of the higher symphony of expanding cosmic life. Songbirds are feathered laureates declaiming the poetry of the skies. Their carols rhyme heights with music. Whether bedded in celestial bowers of blue air or bivouacked in emerald woodlands, their songs are musical bridges linking heaven with earth. When heaven yearns to find a voice, the skylark's minstrelsy becomes that voice. Swallowing a mouthful of sky, he cannot return to earth until that mouthful has been converted into a delicate aria.

A tree rooted in the soil is more than a huge bulk of trunk and branches and leaves. It is the living offspring of earth even as a child is the living projection of its parents' bodies. With knotted arms it embraces the sun, and bathes its brow in pools of moonglow. It communes with the stars across the tremulous stillness of night, and gathers falling rain long enough for naked clouds to replenish their empty wardrobes. Trees are earth's dreams unfolding themselves to the sky.

They are the wooded speech of cosmic themes making conversation with our planet.

Birds, which are tenants both of earth and of heights, have advanced farther than trees in the myriad-chambered mansions of the universe. Their ability to fly permits them to escape the rooted ropes of earth that tether trees to the ground. Having discovered the meaning of freedom, they exultantly dip their wings in sunrise and create a paean to seal this exultation with a hymn. Somewhere in the history of their evolution, they managed to break away from their original complete attachment to their terrestrial environment. Aware of their freedom, they took to the celestial regions and proclaimed their independence by translating into song the rapture that overwhelmed them. Thus becoming the "winged emotion of the sky," they organized the most bewitching choir Nature ever heard.

A bird's throat was fashioned to carry out the sky-born purpose of supernal music. We humans will never understand why a nightingale waits for the onset of darkness before pouring his rhapsody to the stars; but it must stem from some cosmic stimulus to which the bird eagerly responds. Perhaps the darkness is the same companion the sleeping bud fondles before it bursts into flower. There must be a kindred instinct that is common to a bird's singing and a bud's opening. We humans need a light to guide us through darkness; the nightingale needs a song and the bud a stretching into blossom.

Plato seemed to grasp the truth of a universal instinct in songbirds, separate and apart from the miraculous migrating instinct. In "The Laws" he says the theme of joy chorusing in a bird's song reproduces the joyful impulses of the world. Its cantata is an echo of a theme that responds to a timeless baton. It may have been such an idea that gave rise to the legend that the first word God uttered to the world became a skylark. The corollary to this legend would be that God's will is being translated every time a skylark's song becomes vocal.

Every songbird is a courier bearing a fragment of song, and it must deliver its precious script. Music dwells in its delicate throat for the same reason fragrance resides in a flower and warmth in the sun's rays. All are mosaics in Nature's exotic pattern, pulsebeats in the divine poem that began with chaos and ended with Creation. In the final analysis, bird cries may well be the articulated heartcries of earthbound men whose desires yearn to leap skyward out of their song-starved lives.

REVOLT AGAINST PERFECTION

SOME time ago a playwright wrote a play about an American businessman who was killed in an automobile accident. Summoned to the celestial court for judgment, the businessman wondered what the verdict would be. Imagine his elation when he was told, "You are in a place where all is perfect, where all is finished. Here you may have everything your heart desires by merely desiring it. Your wishes will be instantly fulfilled."

He was beside himself with gladness in consequence of his good fortune. Could any mortal have hoped for more? A castle for a house, a bevy of solicitous servants, uninterrupted leisure, complete absence of worry and pain, continuous sunshine—these were now to be his daily diet. Here was perfection indeed.

But eventually dissatisfaction and tedium began to oppress him. All this perfection palled on him. A pronounced nostalgia for something different filled his heart with an unbearable heaviness. He became restless and dejected, whereupon an attendant was assigned to make an investigation. "Aren't you satisfied with this place?" he asked the businessman. "I am thoroughly tired and sick of all this splendor," he replied. "I would like something to do, to explore, something to strive for, yes, even to suffer pain. Here everything is perfection; everything shines with a changeless light; there is never a cloud here; there is never a care of any kind." "Yes, that is true," the attendant agreed. "Here everything is finished; here there are no desires, no conflicts, no yearnings and no hurts." In despair the businessman cried out, "But

I'm tired of all this; I'd rather be in hell." The attendant regarded him with a compassionate look and said, "And where do you think you are?"

Here is a parable that clearly asserts: Where there is perfection there is no room for improvement, and where there is no room for improvement life becomes a stagnant pool. Some religionists would probably dissent on the grounds that perfection is a passport to salvation, and since salvation is an indispensable desideratum for the assurance of immortality, failure to attain perfection is tantamount to eternal doom. This dogma conflicts with Heinrich Heine's terse remark, "Nothing is perfect in this world of ours." A medieval Hebrew poet and philosopher, Moses ibn Ezra, antedated Heine's thinking by more than eight centuries. "Perfection belongs only to God," he wrote. And then he added, "How can you expect me to be perfect . . . when I am composed of contradictions?"

The problem that concerns us here will be considerably elucidated if we make a distinction between "perfection" and "perfectibility." The former is a state of being, and for anyone compounded of flesh and blood, such a state is patently beyond reach. Writing in the *New Republic* almost two decades ago, the American philosopher, Morris R. Cohen, summed it up as follows: "Neither in love nor in work, neither in society nor in solitude, neither in the arts nor in the sciences will the world of actuality permit us to attain perfection."

"Perfectibility" is not a state of being but a process, and as such it occupies not only a valid, but an essential, place in human endeavor. It begins with the premise that man is not and perhaps can never be perfect. But it recognizes man's capacity for self-improvement; more than that, it requires man to make self-improvement the base upon which the superstructure of personality is to be built. A continuous striving after something higher than we are, a conscious and sincere effort to render society and the world better than they are—in this manner we may implement the principle of perfectibility.

The desire to advance *toward* perfection while realizing there can be no actual culmination, the need to master the physical and to become at one with the spiritual—this is perfection as far as man can hope to reach. To know that human life is incomplete and to strive through all our years for its completion—this is the perfectibility within the reach of every human being on earth.

INCE hoary antiquity, when the human mind discovered its capacity for rational activity, man has been asking himself, *"Who am I? What am I?"* He has striven to penetrate the mystery of self, to question the skies overhead, and to shower his deities with oblations, in order to extract an answer. He has attempted to cast furtive glances into the bolted gates of the past, and to lay traps for the unborn future, in the hope of solving the enigma of his own obscurity in the presence of Nature's overmastering forces. The admonition of Socrates, "Know thyself," has never ceased to occupy centrality in the textbook of his mind.

Numerous and varied are the answers given to the query, "What is man?" They range from the cynical declaration that he is nothing more than a chance product of evolution, subservient to the same physico-chemical laws that govern the lowest insect, to the Psalmist's panegyric, "Thou hast made him but little lower than the angels." I trust most of us would dissent from Cowley's view, "Man is too near all kinds of beasts; a fawning dog, a roaring lion, a thieving fox, a robbing wolf, a dissembling crocodile, a treacherous decoy, and a rapacious vulture." For our own self-respect we should undoubtedly prefer the Hebraic view that "On every creature's form there is of God a seal and a token."

A reasonable answer is to be sought somewhere between these extreme views of man. Here is a creature who struts as though he is master of all he surveys, but is felled by a microbe invisible to the naked eye. He swaggers like a colossus, but is impotent like a blade of grass in the presence of a capricious hurricane. He invents and builds scientific instruments to measure the immensities of space and time, but he is utterly lost when attempting to stay the onrushing tide of a single moment.

Oddly enough, it is in these self-contradictions that we may ferret out the pattern of man's true nature. Although he has no illusions about his transiency on this planet, realizing he may be borne away at any moment by unfavorable winds of circumstance, he refuses to regard himself as the plaything of time. He knows he is little more than a temporary jester in the courtyard of mortality, but he snaps his fingers at its imperious rule to which he must ultimately pay final homage. He regards his existence as a trusteeship for a treasure death itself cannot purloin—the fruits of the intellect. He is a channel deeper than the visible phenomena that environ him—a repository of faith. He masters a language more eloquent than any other—music. His heart is a bastion that safeguards life's most sacred reservoir—the wellsprings of love.

In recent years psychology has opened doors for a better understanding of man's ego. It has disclosed a number of personality secrets. But the answer to the title of this essay is still quite remote. Dr. Theodor Reik, the eminent psychoanalyst, makes this observation in his psychoanalytic study, *The Haunting Melody*: "How little we know about ourselves even when we are psychologists, or should I say *especially* when we are psychologists! How seldom we discover what we are really like! A person who seeks to find out will meet an unknown entity. You can have only a blind date with yourself."

But where psychology candidly acknowledges defeat, religion refuses to concede it. *Who am I?* Religion answers: You are a being in whom Deity is unveiled. *What am I?* A conduit through which truth, faith, intellect, love and beauty are siphoned. You were born to soar, to encompass the whole universe with the wings of your spirit. No other destination is worthy of you. Make haste! The years allotted to you are few and of brief duration, but the goal assigned to you is Infinitude. Anoint your spirit with faith and it will teach you how to decipher the idiom of immortality. Thus panoplied, you will be able to see farther than you have ever gazed before. You will look at yourself and see man, but in seeing the man in yourself, you will also behold God's image of which you are a facsimile.

A NEW infant comes into the world. The glad tidings are proclaimed, "It's a boy" or "It's a girl," and happy parents enjoy a foretaste of Paradise.

How tiny, how frail and helpless is the newborn life! The human infant remains dependent longer than any other creature. Its every need must be supplied by elders. Notwithstanding, this fragile sprig of humanity is charged with an inexorable and inescapable mission. It must burst out of its chrysalis of helplessness and defencelessness, and grow into a useful, self-dependent person. The slender thread of early existence must be meticulously safeguarded, to the end that it will develop into a sturdy and vigorous filament of life.

During a child's development, a conventional pattern emerges. It involves four areas to be cultivated: the physical, the emotional, the intellectual and the spiritual. Each is a separate entity, requiring its own specialized treatment. But there can be no whole person unless all four areas make simultaneous progress. The tree of life becomes twisted and warped if any of these branches fails to keep pace with the normal growth of the others. Each is equally indispensable for the proper shaping of personality. All must contribute to the spontaneous activity of the total, integrated individual. Henri Bergson's observation goes to the core of the matter: "Personality is in the very intention of the evolution of life, and the human personality is just one mode in which this intention is realized."

But even after this conventional pattern has been adequately formulated, we must add a further component to render it complete. This component is to be sought in the dimension of *depth*. Life becomes more significant when it is made more profound. There are mountain heights and ocean depths within us, no less than in the physical world in which we live. Height and depth are the systole and diastole of our yearnings and life-throbbings. We are alpine climbers bent on scaling our inner peaks; we are also mariners navigating deeps within our own being that are comparable to the tides and currents churning fathoms above the ocean floor. Beneath the surface of life, according to Carl Jung, one of the world's most astute students of the human psyche, we are inheritors of a "collective unconscious" that began with the first human being who roamed this planet. Our affinity with this "collective unconscious" breaks down the time barrier that constricts our personal lives. Thus, although we live a limited number of years, we are part of a broader life that cannot be walled in by time.

Most persons are so engrossed with the *time* aspect of life that they are oblivious of its equally important *space* aspect. Chronologically, our years are governed by time. But our lives partake of a spatial environment too. Depth is the paramount element in our time-space world. Our movements and actions, our ecstasies and hurts, our upreaching for the Divine and our downplunging into despair—all conform to a height-depth measurement; each registers somewhere on the spatial scale.

But life progresses beyond the limitations of time-space. It advances *above-time* and *beyond-space*. It is continuous and indestructible. It follows an immutable process of always beginning and never ending. It eludes intellectual analysis and logical definition. There it is—like sky and water and air and earth. There it will always be—like love and tears and laughter and pain. It is a process that must be accepted with an ineluctable faith.

Some grow as a bush grows, struggling courageously to

attain maturity, but always remaining lowly in stature. Others grow as a tree grows, rising as if to appease an indefinable height-hunger. But whether as a bush or a tree, time and space are both ivied on every life structure. We must, however, never forget the law of growth that leads beyond these time-space dimensions. It is the dynamic of depth, an imponderable transcending the broken pillars of our bodied clay that must yield to the despotism of time.

HE intellectual history of the human race is characterized by various trends, not the least of which is a fervent quest to differentiate between the true and the false, the permanent and the perishable. Since the infancy of *homo sapiens,* man has felt the need to transfer his allegiance from ephemeral to durable values. Probably without consciously realizing it, he has hungered for stability. He did not fail to observe that practically all the phenomena within his environment and his personal experience paid homage to an inexorable law called change. Nothing seemed fixed. His own cycle of existence—infancy, childhood, youth, maturity, old age and death; the unerring divisions of time—past, present and future; the unfailing rotation of the seasons—spring, summer, autumn and winter; the pattern of his crops—plowing, sowing and reaping; the ebb and flow of the tides; the waxing and waning of the moon; all demonstrated the implacable law of change. This law served as a graphic reminder of the inconstancy of things perceived by the senses. He felt uncomfortable in the habiliments of transiency.

It is not surprising, therefore, that man became obsessed with a yearning to discover, or to create if necessary, something immutable, something unaffected by the caprice of Nature, an enduring component in his life and in the universe. The early Egyptians were among the first to give expression to this need. They strove to translate the principle of permanency to the human body, and out of their striving emerged the amazing art of embalming. This became—so they thought—their immunization to death, their weapon to thwart the tyranny of change. Indeed, they practiced this art with such consummate skill that mummies were preserved in an incredible state of non-decomposition for centuries. Here we have the first known attempt to attain imperishability.

When the mind grew sufficiently disciplined and mature to apprehend abstractions, the concept of permanency shifted from emphasis upon the embalmed body to a belief in the immortality of the soul. The dualism of life, the conviction that man is comprised of body and spirit, and the acceptance of the doctrine of life eternal and of a world beyond this world, furnished a logical stepping stone for the transfer of the notion of changelessness from the body to the soul. Accordingly, some religions affirm that the human soul is a portrait of God, an immortal guest visiting the body for a while, a quintessential entity coextensive with eternity. Though all else be subject to transitoriness, here is something permanent, for it comes directly out of Heaven's repository.

What great comfort mankind has derived from this concept! To be the possessor of an indestructible treasure of divine origin, is to know the ecstasy of the sublimely spiritual in our lives. It is to achieve through spiritual means what the Egyptians sought in the physical realm. Wordsworth's incomparable lines go to the heart of the matter:

> But he who would force the Soul, tilts with a straw
> Against a Champion cased in adamant.

A profound passion to link our temporary finite existence with a higher authority has companioned our race to this very day. It has implanted within us a spiritual venturesomeness whose potentialities for self-improvement are incalculable. We now speak of the infinite in time and space as though infinity and we are twinned. We compute the distance from pole to pole, we measure the spaces from star to star and from earth to interplanetary hideouts. We weigh the sun and saddle its heat and light for our daily use. We proceed to master Nature and to create new blueprints for the future. All this we regard as a normal search for knowledge. But it goes deeper than that. It is the uninhibited longing in man to discover for himself and for his progeny a scaffolding upon which he might construct a mansion of permanence. It is a revolt against the totalitarianism of time, a bid to create during our lifetime some kind of a citadel whose spires will continue to proclaim our presence long after our labors on this earth are ended.

OUT OF THE NIGHT

THE western horizon is laved in a pool of turquoise. Translucent tides of lavender flow almost imperceptibly out of the darkening mists of twilight. As if touched by an invisible magic wand, they melt into a colorful antiphony of lapis and emerald, of pearl and coral. As the canopy of sunglow pales, the weary monarch of day collapses upon his couch, and the sky covers him with a blanket of stars. When the last spent shafts of sunlight are gathered and restored to their golden quiver, a hush that can almost be felt descends upon earth. A cosmic hand draws the purple curtains of the universe and presently the black fog of night comes creeping in.

In this wise we witness night's imperious coronation. Night, with its raven tresses pillowed on the bosom of eternity, hums an alluring chant through the moody silence. Night, beckoning weary men and women to withdraw from the turmoils of day to the lounge of forgetfulness, beguiles their woes with the solacing narcotic of pleasant dreams. Night, a giant hawk swooping through the celestial black ocean, a mammoth charcoal-skinned stag prancing from star to star. Night, a continent of stillness pierced by the sudden cry of a hungry infant calling for its mother's breast. Night, an onyx flask pouring the wine of slumber into the parched lips of many who drank the bitter cup of disappointment all day long. Night—mysterious, entrancing, unfathomable, peering through myriad lids of solitude.

But night tarries not. It slithers along the upper loam for some hours, then beats a hasty retreat when the silver sandals of dawn come tripping down the promontories of the eastern sky. Pausing only long enough to gather up the twinkling goldenrods that bloomed in the planetary garden, it psalms a soft recessional and melts into space. Forests and fields wave emerald ensigns in obeisance to the sun's approaching gilded chariot. Day empties its brimming urns of light upon the last thin layer of nocturnal gauze, and lo—the pendant of sunrise again becomes visible on the throat of the world.

Conceding that man ordinarily prefers day to night, and granting the superiority of day in the portrayal of much of nature's loveliness, I find myself becoming a special pleader for night. I must testify that there is more in night than a vast vacuum created by the flight of the sun. While one can *see* more by day, one can *hear* more by night. During the day man is an extraverted creature, moving noisily about in his daily work. But at night the silence encourages introversion by driving thought inward. It is in such a setting that the voice of the heavens becomes audible; the stillness is an asylum to shut out the boisterousness of the throng, and one becomes aware of a wisdom not to be found in books. Perhaps it was such an insight that moved the author of Psalm 19 to assert, "Night unto night revealeth knowledge." The darkness is an outpost between man and his vanity. Whatever masks were worn by day become utterly meaningless; the calm of night renders them wholly unnecessary. The soul feels chastened and purified because it can see itself without tinsel and without guile.

By day the sun is the single ruler of our planet. In winter we court its light and warmth; in summer we seek to avoid its heat. By night, in the presence of gleaming myriads of suns above us, the world seems more animated, more purposeful and vibrant with life and motion. Contemplating all this grandeur, one cannot help feeling the presence of Deity everywhere. The scars of the earth seem far away, and the distant worlds which are millions of light years away seem to be very near. Only at night can we feel this nearness; we stand on the zenith of our outreaching self and touch the stars.

Out of the night we garner sheaves without stint. The minstrelsies of the nightingale and the serenading recitals of the black-billed cuckoo are an answer to night's necromancy. When I peer into the upper galleries of black sculpture and behold the fascinating skyscapes, I, too, feel an impulsion to pour out part of myself in song.

VERY man is a miniature world reflecting the beauty and glory, the heights and depths, the fruitful fields and lonely deserts of the world that tenants him. He experiences emotional earthquakes and upheavals; he is a heaven for stars of hope and a swamp for slimy pools of greed and jealousy and hate. At times he roams the hilltops of his noblest self; at times he wallows in the dark marshes of sensuality. His mind is a sky where lightning flashes of intuition and intellect dissipate the shadows of ignorance, and unravel new insights concealed from previous generations. At times, too, he is subject to an eclipse; his moral obtuseness blinds him to the aristocracy that requires him to rise above the animal.

Every man's world comprises both land and sea, continents and oceans. Earth and man and sea stem from the same creative source. The human body is about 70% water, and the earth 71%. Science has established that the chemical composition of man's blood is similar to that of sea water. This seems to confirm the scientific hypothesis that life originated in the sea. As for man's affinity with the earth, it is not an accident that the Hebrew word for man and for earth derive from the same etymology—*adamah.* Chapter two in Genesis asserts, "And the Lord God formed man, *ah-far min ha-adamah,* dust from the ground." Into that conglomeration of dust God breathed the breath of life. Into the dust that retained the chemicals and minerals of earth, He injected not only the miraculous phenomenon of life, but also the genius to write poetry, to compose symphonies and to conquer the very elements to which man's clay is wedded.

Not only man and the sea, but also man's depths and sea depths have a common component. Man's unconscious and sub-conscious minds comprise depths many psychological fathoms below his level of consciousness. Likewise, there are depths where the sea floor has dropped some 30,000 feet— 1,000 feet deeper than Mt. Everest is high. The murmur of the surf echoes man's aspirations extending beyond his physical shorelines. The churning tides represent the unceasing inner struggle between the conflicting forces in life that compete to dominate him. Within his restless bosom these tides spurt outward and inward in currents and cross currents.

Most significant in man's miniature world, however, are the thoughts and motivations tabernacled in his brain and in his heart. His thoughts are chariots that transport him to the realm of the intellect. His motivations are the hues that color his relationship to the outer world and to his fellowman. As an individual, he is only a speck of protoplasm, a mite among two and one-half billion other mites scattered upon the face of the earth. His body occupies an area of several cubic feet of space. His duration in time is almost a minus sign when measured by the hoary age of the planet on which he struts like a peacock. His unctuous illusions of self-importance beguile him to pose as a giant rather than as the pigmy he really is.

But what priceless jewels of intellectual creativity and what vast riches of spiritual enterprise he locks in his pigmy breast! Out of the reservoir that is his brain he conjures up visions of immortality. He lives today as though preparing for eternity. Daily he marches closer to the grave, but this does not deter him from reaching out for divine meanings to his brief earthly existence. When Moses ascended Mt. Sinai to receive the tablets of the Law, Scripture affirms that "the Lord came down to meet him."

Climbing Sinai is also part of man's world today. Reaching up for moral tablets to sanctify his own life, he transcends the limited physical precincts that keep him earth-bound, and he becomes the architect of a spiritual domain which spurns death. In this domain he rises above the transiency of his fleeting years. He ascends the ladder of his highest self to meet God, and while ascending, he discovers God descending to meet him in his little world.

LOVE THY NEIGHBOR

THREE thousand years ago, an inspired Hebrew seer gazed into the curtained future and foresaw that the happiness and peace of mankind would depend upon the voluntary observance of a simple admonition: Love thy neighbor as thyself. The principle that motivated the admonition was equally simple: Since your neighbor, like yourself, was created in the divine image, how can you treat him in any way other than you would treat yourself? Your neighbor, even your fellowman, is really you yourself; in everyone resides something of his fellowman. Hence, Love thy neighbor as thyself.

Since there are very few centuries in history that can record the absence of wars, it is quite obvious that the Biblical admonition has been more or less consistently breached. The callous generations of man, incited by the blatant trumpets of greed, malice and fanaticism, have been deaf to this dictum. Their voracious will-to-power prompted them to disfigure the face of history with cruel inhumanities. First with club, battle-axe and bow and arrow; then with spear, sword and massed phalanxes; now with artillery, bombs, intercontinental missiles and atomic explosions, they have inflicted frightful scars on the heart of humanity. Crazed by lust and by the periodic emergence of the savage within him, man permitted his star-beholding mind to become subservient to the law of the jungle. How could the law of love compete with the shrill diapasons of hatred spewed by unconscionable dictators? How can a few uttered words set themselves against the deafening din raised by half-demented would-be conquerors?

It may be argued, and not entirely without justification, that Biblical injunctions are effective when confined to the sphere of homiletics. Self-styled "realists" regard them as theological bromides which lose all effectiveness when they come to grips with grim reality. Too, psychological rules may be invoked to prove that the overmastering instinct for self-preservation renders it utterly impossible for anyone to love a fellowman as himself. Patriotism is a concept a man can understand, because it is comparatively easy to arouse men by thumping the tom-toms of chauvinism. But brotherhood is an abstract idea that must be shared by the heart as well as by the mind. Men grouped together under the aegis of patriotism become armies; men grouped together in a fellowship of brotherhood become a force that converts the human race into a united family. Armies oppose each other, motivated by the law of hate; the legions of brotherhood cooperate with each other while practicing the law of love.

The Hebrew seer who enunciated the dictum, "Love thy neighbor as thyself," is a blood brother of the later prophets who proclaimed that the principles of world-justice and world-brotherhood are the *sine qua non* for world peace. They, in turn, are both the spiritual and the blood brothers of the Rabbis who, some six centuries later, also emphasized the doctrine of the brotherhood of man. One of their number, Rabbi Simeon ben Gamaliel, uttered this trenchant teaching: "The world is founded upon three things—upon truth, upon justice and upon peace." What an appropriate legend this would be for the ensign of the United Nations! A further Rabbinic espousal of brotherhood is implied in the following Midrashic commentary on the verse in Exodus 2. ii, "And Moses went out to his brethren." Eliezer ben Jose remarked, "When Moses went out to his brethren, then the Holy One, God, determined to speak to him." The implication here is crystal clear. Let man go out to seek his brother, and it is a certainty that God's presence will companion Him.

Perhaps some one will venture the opinion that "Love thy neighbor as thyself" is outmoded. If this be so let us, in Heaven's name, become old fashioned. In so doing we may rid ourselves of the blemished wares we have inherited from World War 1 and World War 2. Let us conform to the spiritual doctrine whose preamble reads, "It is better to be the servant of the Lord than the ruler of men."

FROM time to time I ponder with awe the experience of Johann Kepler, the great German astronomer and mathematician of the 16th century. While observing the orbits of the planets and the pathways of the whirling celestial sentinels, his enraptured spirit rose in exaltation when he discovered, among other truths, that a planet's orbit is not round but elliptical. His mind was illumined as by sudden bolts of lightning; it became a receptacle receiving precious fruits from the tree of knowledge. It then dawned upon him that these were not merely isolated facts, but salient thoughts conveyed by a Universal Mind of which his own mental processes were an answering earthly echo.

From that moment Kepler's exploring mind could find no rest. His life became a pilgrimage to track down secrets unrevealed up to his time. In the star-domed empyrean above him he saw not only manifestations of force and movement and matter, but "an Intellect with ideas that were laws and thoughts that were designs." Being deeply religious, his spiritual intuition caught fire. An unalterable conviction persuaded him that this Intellect directing the footprints of the stars and the gyrations of the planets was God. The laws that governed them testified to the wonderful sweep of His power and providence. Clutching the papers on which he had noted his astronomical equations, he sank to his knees as though worshiping at a sacred shrine and whispered tremulously, "O God, I am thinking my thoughts after Thee." Johann Kepler had learned what it means to be in tune with the Infinite.

Kepler's experience has a parallel in the lives of some of us.

There are times when a divine inflow, reverberating within us like a sudden storm, sends us to our knees. We feel a deity in us that breathes a sublime fire into our nostrils, and twins us with the Infinitude that is God's shadow. The pulse within us throbs in harmony with the tempo of the eternal clockwork of the heavens. The geometry of the stars and the geometry of our souls are one. The material universe around us responds to an impulse generated by a cosmic dynamo. But we are sojourners in a spiritual universe that draws exquisite harmony out of the lute of our soul. Its music, being eternal, encompasses all the music that ever was and ever will be. Its ineffable melody evokes a heart rhythm which partakes of the rhythm of the Heart of God. Under the spell of this inner revelation we sink to our knees in genuflection, and like Kepler we cry out, "O God, I am thinking my thoughts after Thee."

Behind and above the pulsebeat of the universe is the Infinite Spirit that animates all. The universe is a partial manuscript of which every human is a syllable. Every life—your life and my life, and all life that ever was and is destined yet to be—comes from the same Source. The dreams we cherish are the waking thoughts and hopes that stem from its Mind. Every blossoming flower, every dazzling snowflake and raindrop, starshine and moonglow, every nightingale's aria filling the theatre of night, every handclasp pledging friendship and every kiss sealing love's betrothal—everything, everything pours out of the flagon of perpetuity. Our lives are stairs ascending the altar-slopes of Infinitude. Though we are of dust and God is everlasting, His Life and our life are linked by the image of Himself stamped upon us at birth.

One who grasps these deeply penetrating truths holds the key to a sublime revelation that is firmly locked in his bosom. It kindles a fire whose first embers caught from a spark greater than any light he had ever known before. It glows like a vestal flame and lights up his whole being. Perhaps he will grope in vain to find a name for it, but even if he fails to come up with a definition, he will know it is a magnanimity that fell into his heart in somewhat the same manner dew-beads spangle the earth before dawn. Dew is the elixir to revive the loam for its matin activity; likewise this new revelation becomes the spiritual unguent that anoints the spirit for the regal role it must play throughout life.

HESE lines are being written on a balcony adjoining my hotel room at San Jose de Purua in Mexico. Forming a massive circular horizon are the jutting peaks of the Sierra Madre mountains. I wonder at what period in the earth's history its interior cooled and shrank away from its outer crust, forming these ridges with their deep canyons and their glittering glaciers. Were these mountains once part of great sea bottoms, rising out of the sea when the earth's crust was pushed to the breaking point?

A little distance below me is a steep ravine through which the Tuxpan River coils like a mammoth snake across moss-covered boulders. Orange groves and banana plantations abound wherever the eye can see, and when their fruits catch the sun they sparkle like golden jewels. Where can one find words poignant enough to describe the beauty of this luxurious tropical paradise? It seems that Nature selected this spot as a site for one of her loveliest temples, and carved these valleys into an urn to hold all the splendor she could gather.

Under my balcony is a cultivated garden ablaze with hibiscus, bougainvillea, many species of roses, fuchsia, calla lilies, and the prolific flamboyante, commonly known as red flame-trees. Some of the blooms grow tall, as if standing on tiptoe to entice the sunbeams to enter their slender bodies. Others heap their floral wares close to the ground, sheltered by the nearness of earth's protective bosom. In the middle of the garden stands a large cactus of the species *Cerei*, towering some thirty feet in the air. Because its branches curve out of a straight, spiny trunk like the outstretched arms of a candelabrum, it is called a candelabra cactus. Birds have pecked openings large enough to build their nests, and under the refuge of these sturdy boughs they hatch their eggs and raise their fledglings.

Daily, with the exception of Sunday, many natives work in the garden from early morn until late afternoon. There they are below me now, their wide sombreros and their colorful serapes protecting them from the scorching sun. Kneeling, sprawling, stooping, often vanishing beneath the heavy foliage, they seem oblivious to everything except the work at hand. For all their labor, I am told, they receive three and a half *pesos* a day, or the equivalent of forty-two cents in American money. The living they eke out is a bare subsistence for their families and themselves. What have they to hoard except their demoralization?

When I contemplate this situation, which exists also in other parts of Mexico, a discordant note jars the melody chorused by these exquisite floral troubadors. Nature's beauty seems desecrated by a human pattern that dooms these laborers to penury. What dividends can they expect to accumulate? What food can their starved souls ever hope to taste? They work silently, almost noiselessly, with steel muscles and strong chests, their wet faces patient and uncomplaining. But what avail them their broad shoulders and strong backs if they must crouch through life at the gateway of poverty? Theirs is a prison within this beautiful Eden constructed by Nature. Their world is a devourer, and they are the devoured. The Talmud teaches, "A laborer may withdraw from his job even in the middle of the day." Should any of these workmen invoke that ancient teaching, they would be without means of support. The strength of the great earth is their strength and the warmth of the benedictive sun is their warmth, but their tables hold only paltry crumbs of earth and sun.

I find myself soliloquizing: why should human beings anywhere be penalized to float like jetsam on the tides of life? Is one mother's son better than another mother's son? Wealth should justly belong to those who earn it. But should human beings be reduced to helpless subserviency as the tools of wealth? God does not hurl life at us like a hunter speeding a bullet towards unsuspecting prey. He hands life gently to each of us like an alabaster cup, to hold both the bitter and the sweet, the wine of dreams and the hemlock of disappointment. But how much of the wine reaches the lips of these natives and their families? Surely, it is not the earth or the sun that relegates them to such a fate. It is their fellowman who is responsible, at least in part, for the blight that extinguishes the fire in the laborer's blood. Men everywhere must be helped to break the chains of destitution that enslave them. No matter what language a man speaks, he must be taught a vocabulary other than that which groans from the tongue of poverty.

Beautiful and warm and kind is Mother earth. There is enough milk in her fruitful body to sustain all her children. Surely, she never intended a few to feast at the expense of the many. She does not discriminate; she is not the architect of the plan that pours honey into some mouths while others drain only the bitter lees left in the bottom of her vats.

Man must learn to be generous as the earth is generous. Earth is the maker of plenitude; man is the creator of poverty. Earth is the builder of fields and groves and orchards and gardens; man builds slums. Blessed will be the human race when man ceases doling out crumbs with one hand while constructing great material empires for himself with the other. Blessed will be man when a profound empathy will impel him to feel the hunger of another as his own and the hurt of another as his own hurt!

HE topography of human life follows a wide arc that extends from earth to heaven. At one extreme is the body, representing the terrestrial tip; at the upper extreme is the soul, representing the celestial point. Each is an accessory to the other; the body as the earthly tenement of the soul, and the soul as the trustee of life after the body has outworn its mundane vestment.

Since the direction of human life, from the point of view both of evolutionary law and of religious upreaching, is from lower to higher, its arc must serve as an escalator to propel man Godward. God Himself serves as the guide in man's journey from earth to heaven. In using the term "heaven" we do not refer to a celestial region which becomes our geographical abode after death. Heaven is the capacity to deserve eternity by virtue of a noble and virtuous life on earth. Here on earth we mount the high towers of heaven and receive a portion of its largess. We build heaven with our lives and with our deeds; earth is the platform on which we stand to erect those towers.

He who is omni-Life deposits an ember of Himself upon the hearth of every human life. This luminous extension of God becomes man's soul and lights up the body until the luminescence returns to its original Source. That which had been God-in-man is then reversed and becomes man-in-God. The cycle is thus completed; the arc is completely traversed.

In consummating this cycle during your lifetime, every person you meet becomes a member of your retinue. You never journey alone from earth to heaven. You are part of an endless caravan, part of a continuous procession which is an invisible dimension of existence. In front of you and behind you, long before you pitched your tent on earth and after you will have pulled up stakes, the trek has been and will always be. Therefore, never fail to reach out your hand to your brother and sister who are marching on the same highway. They need you and you need them. There is no such thing as a "not brother" in the excursion from earth to heaven.

If, when you reach your goal, you find yourself alone, know for a certainty you have lost your way. It is not your brother you have left behind, but yourself. He, like you, is an ember of God, and when you passed him on the road, it was your own soul you bypassed. Nor is it from yourself alone that you have wandered. There is no You except as a tabernacle of God's image; therefore, you cannot turn your back on your fellowman or on yourself without turning away from God.

There is an infallible criterion to guide you toward the Godward road—beat a path to the heart of your fellowman and you will find the Heart of God. You need no other roadmap. Your brother's heart is God's altar, and when you lay upon it offerings of love and understanding, you consecrate the divine familyhood of which God is the universal Father.

The first step in finding your way to your fellowman's heart is to ascend the upward slope of life's arc. But you will never discover the upward slope until you learn also how to gaze downward. He whose eyes are strained toward the upper chambers for a glimpse of heaven will find nothing more than a vacant house with barred windows. Lower your gaze and contemplate your fellow creature below you, for he is the foundation upon which your highest heaven can be constructed. Heaven is not to be found above the curtained canopy of flaming suns and whirling spheres. It exists in a man's heart filled with light for a brother heart in darkness. Heaven is real where a man sated with food and contentment holds out a portion to one who is hungry and in tribulation. Heaven exists where one who is free cannot enjoy his freedom until he helps to sunder the chains binding his brother.

Such a road leads from earth to heaven. Indeed, such a life-direction transforms earth into the highest possible heaven. Here one does not need seraph wings; one's rental for tenancy is only a spiritual mirror in which one is able to see the other as well as himself.

How wide is its spread from wing to wing?
I thought of a bird one day;
And as I stood there pondering,
It rose and floated away.

My years are birds that have swiftly flown,
But I have culled this lore:
The spread of wings remains unknown
Until they begin to soar.

Show me the sweep of your pinions, Soul,
Ascend the farthest sky;
No earthly perch can be your goal,
Remember, remember to fly!

IN THIS brief poem I have striven to voice
an idea that purposes to inspire reflection about the goal of
our mortal existence. It assumes the premise that man is
compounded of body and soul, of intellect and spirit. The
activities of the body are apprehended by the senses, and the
fruitage of the intellect sits enthroned in a man's heart or is
etched upon his countenance. But the soul reveals itself as
inner prophecy; it is the oracle that speaks out of a Burning
Bush whose fire is invisible to our physical organism. Even
as the dimensions of a bird's wings can be ascertained only
when they are poised in flight, so the measurements of a
human soul can be calculated only when an irresistible inner
upreaching renders us aware of an omniscience that goes be-

yond the attainments of the intellect. The soul is not an organ reposing in man; man is the soul's organ. He employs all his functions—breathing, seeing, hearing, willing, thinking; memory, dreams, love, hopes, hands and feet—to carry out the soul's mandate. The soul is the master; it animates all the faculties and functions that make up a man's life. It writes its autobiography upon a man's spiritual scroll with a quill dipped in starshine.

We are rooted in patient earth and our ultimate corporeal couch will be laid in the silent valley. But we have an irrefutable intuition that the soul's quenchless fire defies the burning wick of mortal destiny. The soul-life is not like a star that illumines the ethereal spheres for a while. Rather, it is the mirrored portrait of Deity; it is the channel through which His divine impulses are relayed to us. It is the central commandment issuing from the parliament of heaven, and makes itself known by bridging the human with the divine.

"Remember, remember to fly!" This is the decree the soul promulgates to man. It admonishes him never to forget that, though he is capable of falling to a low estate, he has been entrusted with a hidden compartment where the Highest is always ready to enter. Every excursion into that secret compartment reveals the fabulous riches stored within its vaults. Here he will find wings for his spirit. Here he may attire himself with these wings and outsoar his terrestrial horizons. Here he confronts a never-setting sun, every ray of which is a communication of truth and light. Here the "still, small voice" will whisper prophecies to him, and the whole universe will kneel in rapt awe. Then he knows the highest dwells within him, and he within the Highest.

"Remember, remember to fly!" Once the human spirit learns how to direct its aspiring wings heightward, it discovers pathways whose ultimate destination is eternity. Through such an ineffable experience, our earthly hours become stepping stones to a vision peering through the veil of our physical walls. A new vista, stretching beyond the landmarks of the grave, comes into plain view, and death itself looms as nothing more than a passing shadow. Our deeds on earth become more meaningful and more purposeful, for we shall perform them with the knowledge that some day they will find their place in the soul's treasure house. Not in some hazy other-world, but here on earth and during our lifetime, we shall receive accessions of glory that will shine through the opaque frame of mortality into the higher plane of living which is a giant step in the direction of immortality.

OMEONE aptly remarked that the average man spends most of his life somewhere between a song and a groan. When joy psalms out of us, it is easy to sing with Browning, "God's in His heaven; all's right with the world." But when sorrow and pain flog us with their remorseless whips, we are sorely tempted to voice Shakespeare's lament:

> "Out, out, brief candle!
> Life's but a walking shadow, a poor player
> That struts and frets his hour upon the stage
> And then is heard no more."

The challenge of successful living is met when we learn how to steer a middle course between these two extremes. It is no less precarious to perch oneself on life's highest peaks than to be submerged in life's brooding caverns. A continuous diet of elation, seasoned with monotonous sweetness, is no more digestible than an unbroken fare of pessimism. "Live to seize the pleasure of each passing day," says the epicure. "Live each passing day for the immortality that awaits you," answers the preacher.

The well integrated personality strives to commute between these widely disparate poles. It establishes an acquaintanceship with both, but it does not become a slave to either. Day after day the sun pours its scorching fire upon the naked sands of the desert. Night after night the darkness empties its giant flagons into the swamp of a black emptiness. A full life is possible neither in the desert nor in the swamp.

Neither pain alone nor pleasure alone can be a true compass for living.

Song or groan, life is long when it answers to a great end; it is short when it has no generous task to perform. A single duty achieved between a rising and setting sun may render a life more meaningful than many years spent without earnestness of purpose. Whether we sing or lament, whether companioned by happiness or by adversity, the compelling riddle of life depends on the answer to the question: For what worthy ends am I living?

Because there are many groans in life, many people ask whether life is really worth living. They wonder if there be any rhyme or reason in following the never-ending human caravan as it gropes through life's parched desert in search of crumbs for its unappeased hungers.

Those who raise these questions tell more about themselves than they inquire about life. They reveal how myopic is their perspective and how narrow is their attitude toward the meaning of human existence. They confess an abysmal ignorance of life's major premise, namely, that life is not a matter of choice but of challenge. "Against thy will thou art born and against thy will thou diest," says the Talmud. Any individual who accepts the challenge and renders himself worthy of life's high requirements, never asks if it is worthwhile. But one who looks upon life as an orchard whose fruits he may pluck at will without assuming the responsibilities of its careful cultivation, will soon or late discover the bankruptcy and sterility of his fallacious philosophy.

Often life aches because it is cluttered with too much emptiness. When we probe deeply we become aware of the gaping vacant spaces, and we find ourselves lost in the thoroughfares of our own being. Instead of attempting to fill the emptiness, we accelerate our pace of running away from life by rushing more speedily from ephemeral pleasure to pleasure. But a day comes when we grow weary of flight; we realize we have been pursuing a will-o'-the-wisp. Then the melancholy truth dawns on us that there is a vast difference between "living" and "running." Living means being the hunter; running means being the hunted. The former calls for plunging fearlessly into life's forest, accepting its songs and its groans, bearing its hurts and its joys. The latter calls for taking to one's heels, searching for a non-existent covert where life's groans are silenced.

Song or groan! Whether we sing or lament, in happiness and in adversity, the compelling riddle that cries out of life is this: What am I worth living for?